by Brian Trueman, Edward Cowan and Elisabeth Marks

Purnell

INTRODUCTION

Dear Chaps and Chappesses,

I do hope I'm not too late to catch the post with this introduction – living where I do, of course has its advantages!

I'm jolly pleased you want to join our ranks, though I won't pretend the work is easy! Still, I expect you're young, strong, handsome, brave and super-intelligent like me – otherwise you wouldn't want to be a secret agent in the first place.

Of course, I've grown up in the secret agent business. My mother and father were both secret agents too – part-time, that is. I never knew who they were, naturally. Come to that, they never knew who the other one was and I'm not sure that my father actually knew who *he* was! So I was brought up by a nanny.

Anyway, I digress. Your country needs you and . . . Penfold wanted me to say that it needs him too, but I've sent him to see who that is at the door while I slip in the fact that *no-one* needs Penfold, poor chap! Still, he does make a nice cup of tea.

Good luck with the book. See you at HQ one of these days.

Yours secretly 

ISBN 0 361 05411 4

Published 1982 by Purnell Books Limited, Paulton, Bristol BS18 5LQ
Made and printed in Great Britain by Purnell & Sons (Book Production) Limited, Paulton, Bristol

Acknowledgements:
Edited by **Elisabeth Marks**
Designed by **Rob Burt**
Illustrations by **Peter Campbell, Michael Wells Studio** and **David Farrah**

DANGERMOUSE

There is **no** official profile on D.M. There are one or two memos relating to his activities but even these are written with invisible ink and, if they **are** ever typed up, it is done by a blindfold typist in a blacked-out dustbin who types on invisible paper with a keyless typewriter.

These records are difficult to come by. All one can say for sure is that .... de .... is not his real name — any more than Dangermouse is his real code name.

Any references to our hero, then, can only be drawn from the unofficial biography by Gerbil de Gook (Published Robin Matchbox & Co., 1976.)

What follows is a summary (though written in winter) of the early chapters:

Dangermouse's father is thought to have been of noble birth, considerable girth and little worth — though, as an amateur inventor, he is credited with devising the Cheadle Hulme portable tennis elbow (still obtainable from some of the more provincial retail outlets of Her Majesty's Stationery Office).

On his mother's side — and not many people were — his ancestors were all leaders of men except for the Black Sheep of the Family who was a sanitary engineer and the likely source of the famous legend of the Woolly Black Plumber of Ramsgate.

In the year of his birth his mother joined the ill-fated Cutt-Pryce Everest Expedition. Apart from D.M.'s mama, the expedition included Mr. U. L. Tyde, famous in his day for his Chippendale wooden leg. One evening, after a hard day struggling with cravats and glaziers, they were resting at Camp 3, somewhere between 22,000 and 22,004½ feet above sea level (the sea was rough at the time).

Though it was bitterly cold, the heavily pregnant Mrs. .... de .... was warm enough as the one-legged climber had donated a spare artificial limb and the U. L. Tyde leg was blazing cheerfully in the cold darkness of the night.

In the leader's tent, U. L. had joined Cutt-Pryce in a drink. "Blast!" grunted the Colonel. "This sherry's cold! Pass the loofah, there's a good. . ." Suddenly, he broke off.

"Oh blow!" ejaculated Tyde. "There goes our last chance of winning the gold for that great country of ours in the three-legged race!" Then, in the eerie stillness, a tiny wail drifted over those icy peaks.

"What, in heaven's name, is a tiny whale doing this far above sea level?" cried Cutt-Pryce.

"No, no, Colonel, it's . . . it's . . . Dangermouse!" whispered Tyde in awe. The next morning the Lt. Col. was drawing on his pipe after breakfast.

But before he could call Sherpa Fivesing — Sherpa Tensing's half-brother — Dangermouse, always a precocious child, pushed his head into the tent. "Mind if I join me, Colonel?" he called cheerfully, and seconds later he pushed his body into the tent

"That's it!" he smiled. "Planted the flag on the top. I'm just popping down to Katmandu for a quick interview then I'll be back for the Mater!"

By the time the rest of Cutt-Pryce's team had reached the plains, the population of Katmandu had learned of the birth of Dangermouse on the Magic Mountain and of how he had conquered the peak.

"A little older in years," said the Mayor of Katmandu, "and he will undoubtedly be conquering more Pekes and a Wire-Haired Fox Terrier!"

In September that year, young Dangermouse started at Eton after which he went on to Cambridge, Oxford, Harvard, the

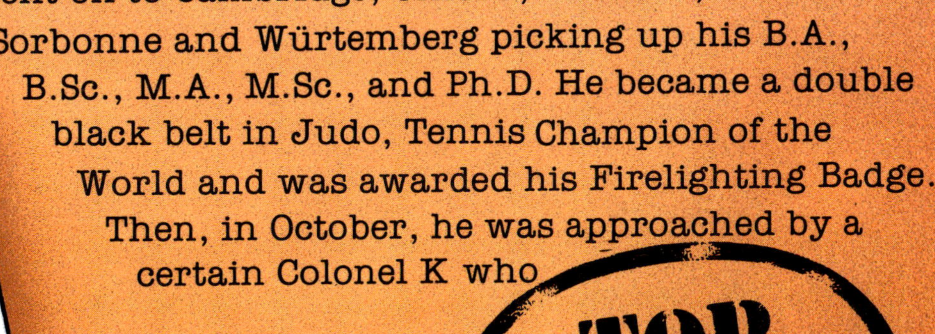
Sorbonne and Würtemberg picking up his B.A., B.Sc., M.A., M.Sc., and Ph.D. He became a double black belt in Judo, Tennis Champion of the World and was awarded his Firelighting Badge. Then, in October, he was approached by a certain Colonel K who

TOP SECRET
CENSORED

(Wilbraham Keith Benedict).

Only son of Arthur Wigglesworth Penfold and Bronwen Merionedd Ysptty Ystwyth Penfold (née O'Herlihy).

Place of birth: Osbaldestone Bottoms, Lancashire. Moved to Plumstead, S.E. London, when 7 months old.

One of a long line of family of HAMSTERUS COWARDISSIMUS TERRIFICATUS — recognisable by the broad yellow stripe down the centre of the back.

Distantly related to the Dutch hamster who reported a burst dam when his garden spade hit a water pipe. This caused a panic evacuation of the city — traffic ground to a total standstill causing the original hamster jam.

Educated at short notice and Whipsnade. Always of nervous disposition, took correspondence course in 'How to Overcome Fear' but failed to complete because too scared to go out and post papers.

Memo
From: Internal Investigation Branch
To: Colonel K.
Subject: Penfold (code name: Penfold) (Code name's codename: Jigsaw — Because he goes to pieces in a crisis. D.M.)

We have now completed our investigation into the circumstances under which the above was taken into service.

In early March 1980 he was shopping in Mr. Dorian Pamp-le-Mousse Jones' greengrocery establishment in Firebrick Road, Willesden Green.

Eye witnesses spoke of high-pitched complaints from the subject when Mrs. Anastasia Jones sold a cauliflower he had been hiding behind. He dived into the till and attempted to conceal himself beneath a pile of pound notes. Attached is Mr. D. P. Jones' statement.

Statement by .... de ....
(Code name: Dangermouse)

I'd just finished playing Mendelssohn's Violin Concerto in the lotus position with one hand tied behind me — at least, I **think** it was behind me, chatting to K on the videophone — when I heard an odd noise — a sort of squealing bump.

"Good grief!" I said to myself and opened the sitting-room door. Whatever it was lying there had come from top to bottom — down three flights of spiral staircase.

It just lay there crumpled and torn, flat as a pancake, pale brown with battered edges. Paper bag didn't look too good either!

So — I took the poor thing in, showed him where the ...... is, how to maintain the ...... and key secret agent know-how like cleaning the car, pressing my suits, and polishing the eye-patch.

And he's jolly useful. The slightest whiff of danger and he's off like a rocket.

Statement by D. P. Jones

At about 'alf past ten in the mornin' of March tenf I'm floggin' greens as per usual when I 'ears this flippin' squealin'.

"Shurr up!" I says to the trouble[1], "or I'll motorway[2] yer in the norf[3]!"

"Don't give me yer sailin'[4]!" she says, "or I'll Fleetwood[5] yer minces[6]! Besides," she says, "I never oranged[7]. It's this little Scrooge[8] 'ere!"

So I takes a boatman's[9] in the Jack[10] and sees the little feller.

"Whatcha want?" I says.

"T-t-t-t-two pounds of p-p-p-p-potatoes," 'e says. So I finds a two-pounder among the King Edwards and I says:

"Howzat?" At that 'e jumps about six feet in the air an' disappears inside a brown paper bag.

"It's a **nice** pertater!" I says "Come out an' make friends."

Would 'e come out? No chance! In the end, the trouble[1] 'ad a bright idea.

We gets 'is address, writes it on the bag, sticks a slopin'[11] on it an' gives it to the errand boy ter post.

KEY TO STATEMENT BY D. P. JONES

1. Trouble and strife = wife
2. Motorway smash = bash
3. North and south = mouth
4. Sailing ship = lip
5. Fleetwood Mac = black
6. Mince pies = eyes
7. Orange peeled = squealed
8. Ebenezer (Scrooge) = geezer
9. Boatman's hook = look
10. Jack and Jill = till
11. Sloping ramp = stamp

COLONEL 'K'

K, Colonel (real name: Category Delta Plus).

Born: Probably.
Place: Malaysia.
Father: Hon. Quentin Ascot Shoetree Knight-Knight Sleepwell, Bart.
Mother: Hon. Lady Amaryllis Hippeastrum Forfar-Fife.
Education: Two Scout badges (Sleeping and Macramé) C.S.E. Plasticine work B.A., M.A., M.Sc., Ph.D., University of East Dukinfield.
Graduated: Plumpton Worswick Academy of Sheep-Spotting.
1934/35: Taught Chemistry, Old Dripping-on-Toast Grammar School, Gloucestershire. School burned down Spring 1935.
1935/36: Taught Physics, Swottencram Academy, Glen Sprocket, Aberdeenshire. Staff and pupils electrocuted March 1936.
1936/37: Taught Rugby, Brewing and Needlework, Plas Twryffparys Secondary School, Glamorganshire.
1937/39: Various independent activities of scientific nature: Fiduciary interchange friction igniting devices; Waterloo Station.
1939: Enrolled in Intelligence Corps. Oct.
1946: Controller, Intelligence. Relieved of overall responsibility — as too many overalls came back half size and minus buttons.

Report on Investigation into Agent K's possession of unauthorised supplies—namely one portion of chips—with criminal intent.

Agent K was taken to HQ—via Banbury Cross, Waltham Cross and King's Cross—so he could be cross-examined.

Over three days of intensive questioning he resolutely denied that the portion of chips in his possession—bought from a fried food establishment in Aldershot—was intended to accompany the grilled goldfish obtained from the blazing home of Lt.-Col. Douglas Lee-Enfield Twentie-Mill Howitzer.

Even when given the Chinese Burn, threatened with School Dinners and the confiscation of his prize conker he refused to change his story and denied that he ever planned to eat the said goldfish.

I am therefore convinced of his innocence and recommend early release.

S.P. ff-ff. WK
Deputy Head Intelligence Corps

Memo **Department of Intelligence**

From: **M**
To: **STC**
Subject: **K**

Look here! What's all this dam' nonsense about this chap bein' no use?

Haven't you read his fishing record? 24 trout caught with a fly he tied himself. He also landed two 38lb salmon and a pram wheel just the right size for me golf trolley.

And he's a member of the Anathema—best club in London. Plays a jolly good game of golf, too—I only **just** beat him.

Stop fiddlin' about! Take him on at once and get him made up to Colonel immediately!

DANGER MOUSE
WHO STOLE THE BAGPIPES?
THE SCOTTISH HIGHLANDS WHERE HERDS OF BAGPIPES GRAZE PEACEFULLY UNDER THE WATCHFUL EYES OF THE BAGPIPE GILLIES. BUT WHAT IS THIS? WHY ARE THE EVIL HENCHMEN OF BARON GREENBACK ROUNDING THEM UP?
HEADA DEM UP! MOVA DEM OUT! YAHOO!
MEANWHILE BACK IN MAYFAIR...
CHIEF, WE'RE WANTED.
WELL, DON'T JUST STAND THERE! TO THE CAR!
OUR HEROES WERE SOON ZOOMING THROUGH LONDON WHILE COLONEL K BRIEFED THEM ON THE TV MONITOR.
COLONEL K TO DANGERMOUSE! COME IN! ARE YOU THERE? DRAT THESE NEW-FANGLED CONTRAPTIONS! ONLY HAD CARRIER PIGEONS WHEN I WAS IN THE FIELD.
DANGERMOUSE HERE, SIR.
OH, THERE YOU ARE! GOOD SHOW! NOW THERE'S NOT MUCH TIME – GET YOURSELF UP TO SCOTLAND. SOME BLIGHTERS RUSTLING BAGPIPES.
BAGPIPES, SIR? WHO'D WANT TO DO THAT?
ANY MEMBERS OF A MUSIC APPRECIATION SOCIETY WHO CAN'T TAKE ANY MORE!
MEANWHILE, ON A RUGGED PEAK, THE OCCUPANTS OF A SINISTER ROBOT STAG WERE WAITING.
JUST AS I THOUGHT! THEY'VE SENT THAT WITLESS WHITE WONDER, DANGERMOUSE, TO STOP ME! STILETTO! IS EVERYTHING READY?
SI, BARONE!
DANGERMOUSE AND PENFOLD WERE SHOWN TO A ROOM WITH A VIEW IN McNASTY'S LOCH NESS HOTEL.
AYE WELL. YOU'LL BE NICE AND COSY HERE AND THE WINDOW GIVES THE BEST VIEW OF THE LOCH IF YOU BE WANTING TO WATCH FOR THE MONSTER! GOODNIGHT.
YOU KNOW, SIR, I DON'T LIKE THE LOOK OF THAT McNASTY CHAP. IT WOULDN'T SURPRISE ME IF HE WAS OUT THERE NOW, SIGNALLING TO SOME VILLAIN TO AND GET US – MAYBE EVEN THE LOCH NESS MONSTER.
FOR A HAMSTER. YOU'VE CERTAINLY A VIVID IMAGINATION, PENFOLD.

BACK INSIDE THE STAG...
EH, BARONE! THERE'S THE SIGNAL FROM MCNASTY.
GOOD! NOW LET'S SEE WHAT DANGERMOUSE MAKES OF MY MECHANICAL LOCH NESS MONSTER. HEE HEE HEE!
FROM THE SAFETY OF THE LOCH SIDE DANGERMOUSE AND PENFOLD WATCHED THE MECHANICAL MONSTER MAKE MATCHWOOD OF MCNASTY'S HOTEL.
GOOD GRIEF! WHAT A STROKE OF LUCK! IF YOU HADN'T PERSUADED ME TO GO MONSTER WATCHING WE COULD BE UNDER THAT LOT!
CRIKEY! YES! BUT WHERE'S MCNASTY?
UP HERE, YOU SASSENACH! GET ME DOON!
NOT UNTIL YOU TELL ME WHERE GREENBACK IS.
I'LL TELL YE! HE'S UP AT CASTLE MACSTRANGLE WITH 10,000 BAGPIPES.
ALRIGHT, HANG ON! WE'LL GET A LADDER. COME ON PENFOLD.
WHERE DO YOU THINK WE'LL FIND A LADDER, DM?
AT CASTLE MACSTRANGLE. MCNASTY'S ALRIGHT. HE'LL HANG AROUND UNTIL WE GET BACK.
STRANGE SOUNDS EMERGED FROM CASTLE MACSTRANGLE.
THE SOUNDS WAVES FROM TEN THOUSAND BAGPIPES AMPLIFIED THROUGH MY SONIC CANNON WILL CREATE A RAY POWERFUL ENOUGH TO DESTROY ANY BUILDING!
DANGERMOUSE DREW UP OUTSIDE THE CASTLE.
OH, WHAT A SHAME, THE FRONT DOOR IS LOCKED. LOOKS LIKE WE'LL HAVE TO GO BACK EMPTY HANDED.
PENFOLD, SHUSH. I'LL EJECT MYSELF IN AND THEN PULL YOU ACROSS.
THERE MUST BE AN EASIER WAY OF MAKING A LIVIIIIIING!

INSIDE GREENBACK PREPARED TO ACTIVATE HIS WEAPON
NOW, NERO, ALL IS READY AND NO-ONE CAN STOP US. HEE HEE! I CAN'T DECIDE WHICH CITY TO DESTROY FIRST.
YOUR CONCERT IS CANCELLED, BARON
YOUR NEXT FEW YEARS WILL BE SPENT BEHIND BARS.
ME? BEHIND BARS? OH, NO DANGERMOUSE, NOT ME– YOU! STILETTO! A CAGE FOR OUR GUESTS.
DON'T WORRY, PENFOLD WE'LL SHOOT OUT OF HERE IN A JIFFY.
NOW RELAX AND ENJOY THE ENTERTAINMENT. STILETTO! SHOW OUR GUESTS TO THE BEST SEATS! HA! HA! HA!
PRECARIOUSLY PERCHED ON A ROCK FACING DOWN THE CAVERNOUS CANNON BARREL THERE SEEMS NO HOPE FOR THE HEROES.
DID I EVER TELL YOU WHY I NEVER BECAME AN OPERA SINGER, PENFOLD?
NO! AND RIGHT NOW I'M NOT REALLY BOTHERED, DM!
WHEN I SANG THE HIGH NOTES THINGS USED TO BREAK- NOT JUST GLASSES— ANYTHING.
SO WHAT?
DANGERMOUSE'S HIGH FALSETTO BROKE THE CHAINS THAT HELD THEM. BUT, WAS IT TOO LATE? ALREADY THE SONIC RAY WAS SPEEDING TOWARDS THEM.
THAT THING'S GETTING AWFULLY CLOSE, WHAT SHALL WE DO, DM?
WELL, FIRSTLY, I'D SAY DUCK! WE'LL TAKE IT FROM THERE.
THE BEAM BOUNCED OFF THE ROCKFACE JUST ABOVE THEIR HEADS AND SHOT BACK TOWARDS THE CASTLE. A HUGE EXPLOSION SENT BAGPIPES FLYING EVERYWHERE.
BACK IN MAYFAIR...
GOOD SHOW THAT SCOTTISH AFFAIR, DM. ONE THING PUZZLES ME, THOUGH. BARON'S CASTLE BLEW UP A WEEK AGO WHERE HAVE YOU BEEN SINCE?
WELL, IT TOOK A LONG TIME ROUNDING UP ALL THOSE BAGPIPES. THEY'RE ALL SAFELY GRAZING NOW— EXCEPT ONE. PENFOLD! PIPE DOWN!

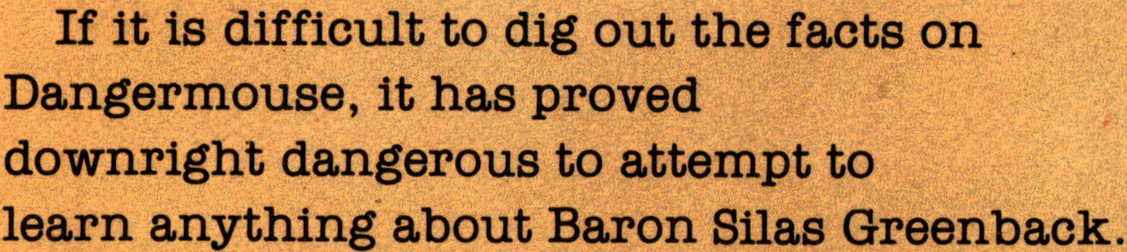

If it is difficult to dig out the facts on Dangermouse, it has proved downright dangerous to attempt to learn anything about Baron Silas Greenback.

What he is, is common knowledge. At the mention of his name, tyrants tremble, strong men go pale and hard-boiled eggs turn to jelly.

But such is his power that no computer holds a single fact on him or his origins. He pays no income tax — who would dare collect it? He drives without a driving licence, shoots without a gun licence and keeps a pet caterpillar without a pet caterpillar licence. Nevertheless, infinite pains (mostly other people's) have been taken to uncover the background to the Terrible Toad and what few documents are available are attached.

DOCUMENT GB/1 **Report from Agent H17/E/4938765/i/ECK**

I have now spent 17 days in the Willesden stake-out. I shall be glad to get back to beans on toast again.

It is clear that Greenback is communicating with the underworld through an ingenious and complicated code. He places messages in an ordinary domestic container outside the door of his HQ and these are collected by a messenger in the early hours of each morning.

The trained goldfish provided by control has failed to return from a retrieval mission across Willesden Green High Street. However, I succeeded in photographing three of these secret messages by disguising myself as a garden path and after treatment for an attack of gravel, I despatched these yesterday to Major CXkkp3N, Head of Ciphers.

Must finish. Suspect am being watched. Reason to believe that Greenback is none other than. . . . . aagh!

Document GB/2

From: CXkkp3N To: K. Subject: Cifers, Ciphuz, Cyff, Codes

1. **3 Sat + 1 lge Cr. none Fri. Ta**
This is straightforward stuff. The blighter has got hold of super-classified info about our missile strength! 3 SATURN inter-continentals and 1 large CRUISE MISSILE. He's also latched on to our delivery difficulties with the new cataclysmic, laser-equipped sock-melting FRIGHT missile.

Had some difficulty over who TA might be but now sure it's Tamariscifolia Azimuth, the defective Balkan agent.

2. **4 Wed**
At first my chief aide, 33TWiTT, linked this with the installation of **W**estmacott **E**xponential **D**ishwashers in the House of Commons Cafeteria.

The only thing that didn't tie up was the '4'. Cut-backs have meant the H. of C. has only 3 WEDS.

Then it dawned — it's an instruction to waiting troops, poised to attack. For '4 WED' read 'FORWARD'. Simple.

Only problem is where are they and who are they going to attack?

3. **No Milk Today, Three Pints Tomorrow**
This, key evidence, is quite different — and written in a different hand. By analysing the paper, the fingerprints **on** the paper, the ink **and** the encoded message, I have been able to crack the real identity of Silas Greenback.

It is **so** astounding that I have told no-one until now. Greenback is none other than .... hang on, someone at the door.

"Yes? Ah, come for the milk money, have you? Just a moment while I get my .... aaaagh!"

Editor's Note:

A few hours before the presses started to roll on this unique publication, a swarthy, raincoated figure with a large nose carrying a machine-gun case arrived at my office. Opening the case, he took out a violin and threatened to play if we did not publish the contents of a letter he bore. There are some things beyond human endurance. So we rushed it into print. Here is that letter:

"Fools, Peasants and Brats,

So, you dare to meddle in my affairs! Who I am and what my noble birthright is, is no concern of yours! I am great – the greatest evil genius in the world! Kneel before me and confess me king!

By now you will have found the packet enclosed with this letter which I am dictating to Stiletto.

In one minute's time you will be eliminated since I have included a bomb which will send you to your death!

Wait! Stiletto! What is that on the mantelpiece? You dolt! You forgot the bomb – unfortunate wretch! Aaaaagh! Boooom!!!"

STILETTO

Nasaccio Mafiosa Cornetto — to give him his real name — was born in the little walled Italian town of Semolina di Budino.

"Rigoletto!" exclaimed his mother as the midwife pressed him into her arms, "but he is — a beautiful! Look Juan!" (His father was the famous Italian lawyer 'Just' Juan Cornetto.) "Look! He has the handsome black feathers of a crow and the mouth of a jackdaw!"

O.K!" said Papa. "If you say so!" And taking the infant, he hurled him into the garden.

"Osso bucco!" screamed Mrs. C. "I said 'feathers of a **crow** and the **mouth** of a **jackdaw**' — not 'throw him out of the back door!' "

Meanwhile, as the infant Stiletto was lying howling among the spaghetti bushes, a pair of wolves called Ron Miller and Remould passed by and lobbed the cheeping infant back into the house by way of the letter box.

It was then that Stiletto decided to devote his days to the devious double dealing and disgrace of a desperado.

Soon after these events, he was spotted by one of Greenback's scouts as he stole babies' rattles in the Piazza di San Marco and recruited into his organisation.

Greenback realised, as soon as Nasaccio signed on the bent dotted line, that he had a right-hand man worthy of his evil.

He was, as the Baron said, "One of the sharpest little heels the world has ever seen — we shall call him Stiletto!"

NERO

Instar Emperor Nero the Second of Chorlton-cum-Hardy.

Author of the best-selling guide to an insect-dominated society: "The Pest Decides".

Nero comes from a long line of Champion Caterpillar at Tufts. The species, CREEPIO NASTISSIMUS, is noted for its evil intelligence, its loyalty to criminal geniuses and its cunning attempts to overthrow all that is good.

At an early age Nero sold his own moth-er to a butterfly farm.

In 1979 a top level enquiry was launched into the mysterious disappearance of valuable roses from Colonel K's garden in Chorleywood. All the evidence pointed to the rosenap being the job of an eight-man gang.

Traces of white hair and mysterious semi-circular bite marks on the leaves made Nero a prime suspect. The eight separate sets of footprints, however, clearly eliminated him from the enquiries (since Nero presumably doesn't have any feet).

It was not until early 1981 that D.M. was able to penetrate Greenback's hideout by ingeniously allowing himself to be frozen into a block of blackcurrant-flavoured ice.

It was when Nero opened the door of the fridge to have a quick lick that D.M. was able to solve the mystery.

Twenty-four hours later D.M. was explaining to Colonel K.

"N-N-Nero, sir! Th-th-that's why we n-never kn-kn-kn-knew he had s-s-s-sixteen feet! He w-w-w-wears eight p-p-pairs of m-m-m-moon boots — w-w-white furry . . ."

MAKE YOURSELF

No, Penfold, you may not start off this section! Chocky bickies are *not* part of a normal spy kit, nor is the mouth a good hiding-place for any part of the kit.

Please remember that you have pouch cheeks – cheeky with it! – so you have an advantage over our readers!

Every good spy should be well equipped. In your kit you will need invisible ink and a pen for writing secret messages, a code book for writing and deciphering messages, simple instant disguises – make up, a burnt cork for moustaches and 'black teeth' (Penfold swears by these but I simply remove my eye patch. It always fools Penfold. He never recognises me), candles for secret writing and a small compass.

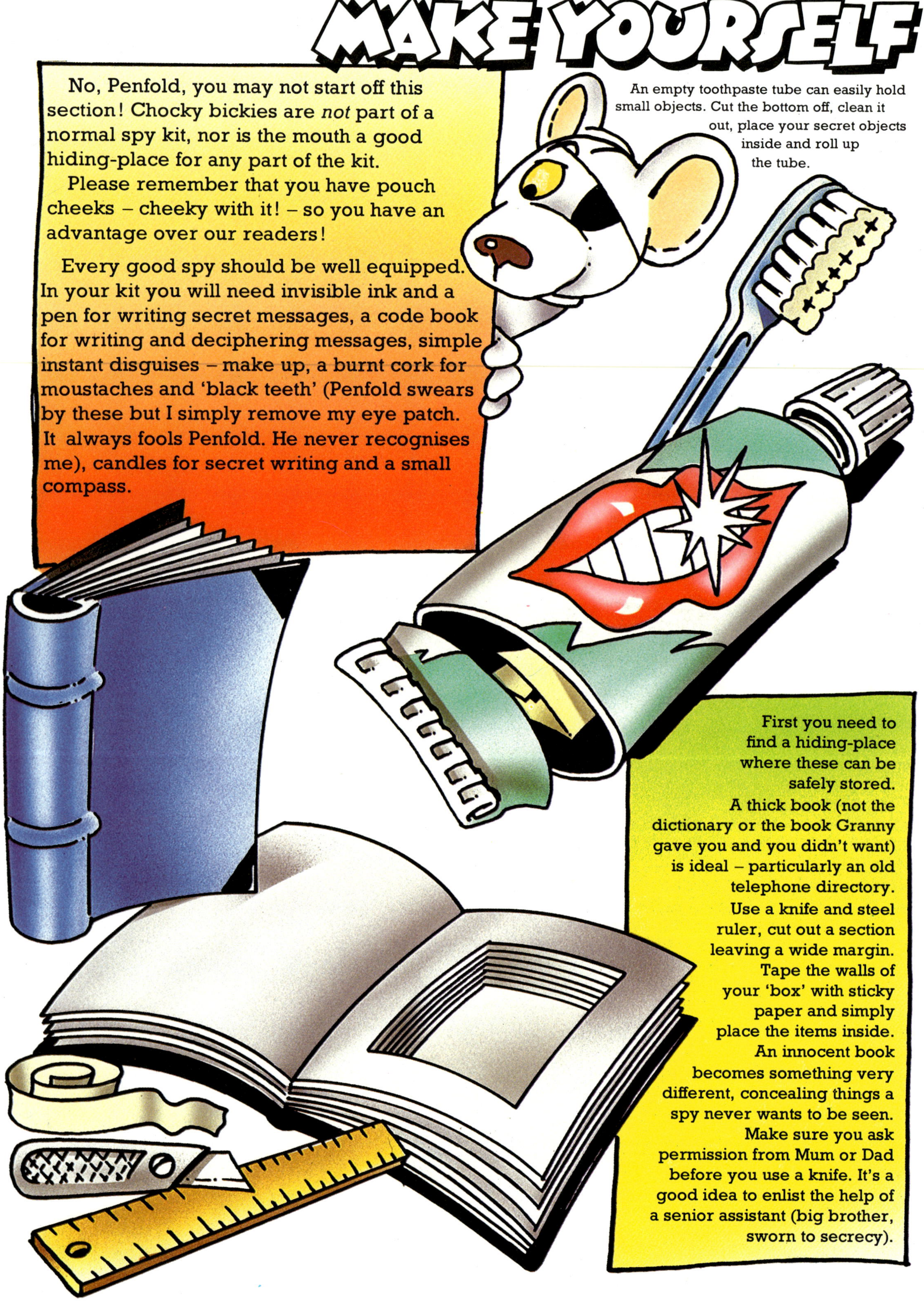

An empty toothpaste tube can easily hold small objects. Cut the bottom off, clean it out, place your secret objects inside and roll up the tube.

First you need to find a hiding-place where these can be safely stored.

A thick book (not the dictionary or the book Granny gave you and you didn't want) is ideal – particularly an old telephone directory.

Use a knife and steel ruler, cut out a section leaving a wide margin.

Tape the walls of your 'box' with sticky paper and simply place the items inside.

An innocent book becomes something very different, concealing things a spy never wants to be seen.

Make sure you ask permission from Mum or Dad before you use a knife. It's a good idea to enlist the help of a senior assistant (big brother, sworn to secrecy).

a SPY KIT

1 A matchbox makes a useful pocket spy kit.

2 Paste a few matches onto a piece of card to make a false bottom.

3 Put a mini pencil, candle and your secret messages in the box.

4 It will look like an ordinary box of matches attracting no suspicion.

Remember, anything a spy uses must look very ordinary and inconspicuous. It must always seem to be what it is not.

For instance, the toe of a football boot can make a safe hiding place for small items. Wedge securely in place with cottonwool.

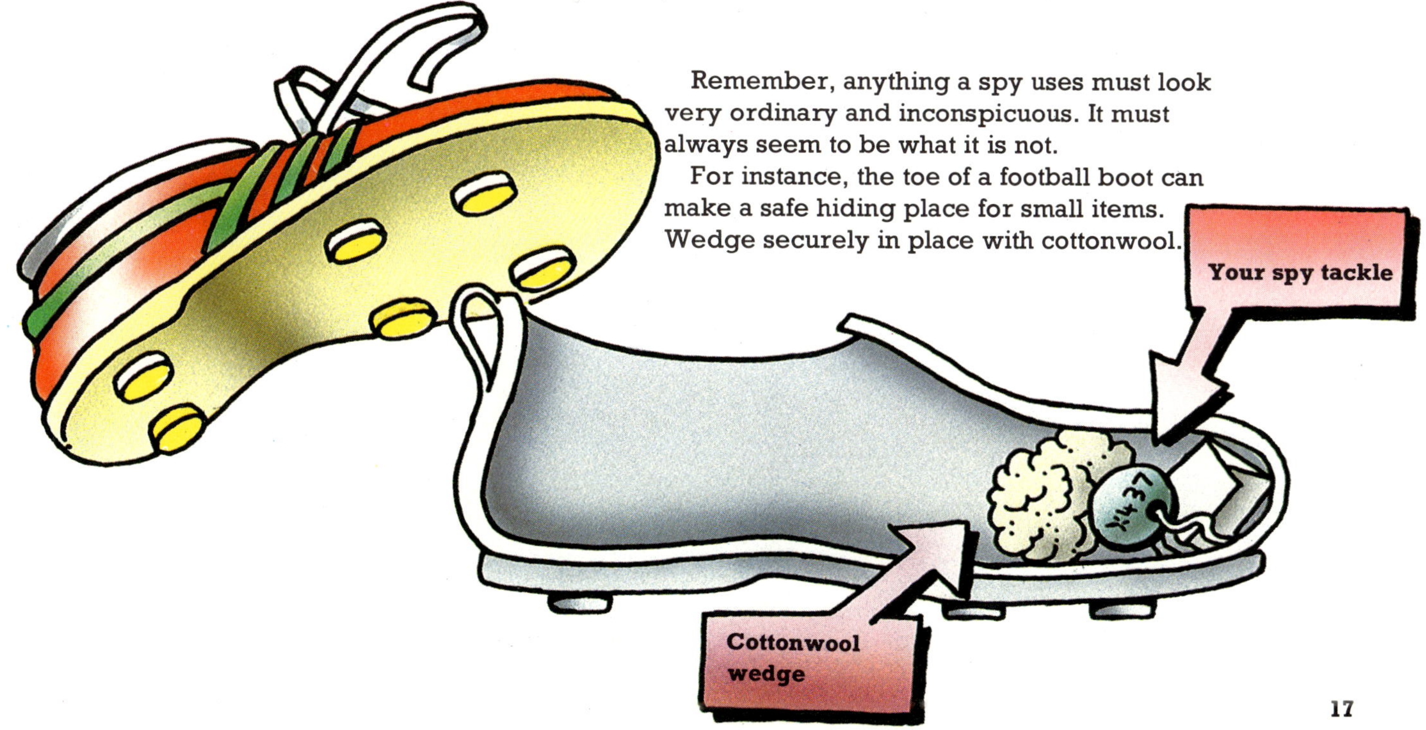

London – home of the Beefeater and the costermonger; home of the Pearly King, home of commerce and trade, and home (in a typical Mayfair pillar box) of the world's greatest detective – the one and only Dangermouse!

It was 7.30 a.m. one April 33rd and Penfold faced his chief and swung a karate chop at him.

"Oh, for goodness sakes!" he exclaimed. "Not so soon after my boiled egg!"

At that moment the alarm bleeped on the videophone.

"That'll be Colonel K!" said Dangermouse

"Ah, Dangermouse," said K. "Got a problem only you can solve! Just take a look at this."

"Gosh, Colonel!" said Dangermouse. "That's the Big Ear Tracking Station!"

"Exactly – keeps tabs on every villain in the world. And, DM," said Colonel K, "it's told us that someone's going to steal it!"

"The Big Ear? – that's aiming high, sir. It'll destroy the global network! But who would do . . . ?" Dangermouse began.

"I'll show you," said K – and pressed another button. "I'm afraid it's your old enemy – Baron Silas Greenback. His Frogs Head Flyer was spotted near the Big Ear yesterday! He's gotta be stopped, DM!"

"Never fear, Sir," averred Dangermouse courageously. "Right, Penfold – come on . ."

It was several hours later, as they streamed silkily over the ocean that Penfold spotted a large signpost.

"Enter at your own risk," he read. "Enter *what* at your own risk, Chief?"

"The Bermuda Triangle!"

"Cor!" said Penfold, "I used to play one of those in the school band!"

"The *Bermuda* Triangle," groaned Dangermouse, "is where ships and aircraft vanish without trace! Some blame flying saucers – utter rubbish, of course. What's our position, Penfold? Penfold?!"

He turned to see why his assistant didn't reply – and in no time at all his ice-cold brain had come up with an answer – he wasn't there!

"There's a logical reason for his disappearance, of course," murmured the White Wonder. "It's just that I can't think what it is! Ah well – better turn back and search, I sup . . ."

But then, a strange thing happened. The lights on the instrument panel lit up with a strange green light and the cigar lighter played God Save the Queen in the wrong key as the Mark III was bathed in an odd golden glow.

He stopped abruptly. There, hanging in the air was the Greenback Flier. Its speaker crackled into life.

"Come to spoil my plans eh?" boomed the awful voice of Baron Silas Greenback. "I think not, White Wonder!"

Dangermouse didn't hesitate a second. He rolled, looped, added a Falling Leaf to an Immelman turn and swept low over the sea, with the Baron in hot pursuit.

"Curses and drat!" snarled the toad. "He's out-manoeuvring us. Stiletto, launch the homing missile!"

"Si, Barone!" called his henchman.

DM was congratulating himself on his getaway when . . . "Oh-oh! It's a homing missile! Good grief! *This* is going to need some fancy driving!"

"Where am I!" cried our hero. "Good grief, he's sucked me into the Frog's Head Flyer! All right, Greenback, do your worst! I . . . Wow!"

Before he could finish his challenge, he was sucked up into a vast tube that hung above the car. Momentarily, he blacked out and when he came to it was to find himself strapped to a table in a seemingly deserted operating theatre.

"Me and my big mouth!" he groaned. "Look, Greenback – I'm not going to take this lying down!" There was no answer to his cry, but through a swing door entered a small, weirdly clad figure.

"Oh good show! Room service!" joked Dangermouse bravely, "I want to complain about this bed – I can't get out of it! And you can take that silly mask off."

"Szzuzzh!" came the response. "Stay unmoving earthling, or you will be rendered harmless!"

"*Arm*-less!" exclaimed Dangermouse. "Don't fancy that – they stop my shoulders fraying!"

The White Wonder turned his head – as far as he could – and all at once saw that a gallery ran round the whole theatre. What was more, it was packed with creatures dressed more or less exactly like the first. This one spoke again:

"Zock speaks! Pay attention class! This is a prime specimen of what the earthlings call 'a hero'. Watch the tests carefully – I

will be asking questions at the end of the lecture!"

"What *is* this?" asked Dangermouse, witheringly. "The Greenback Supporters' Club outing?"

"First I shall take the body readings in the usual way ..."

The creature, Zock, touched small illuminated panels on a gleaming control unit. There was a whirr – and long metal arms extended and proceeded to pinch, punch and pummel our hero.

"Ow! Oof! Hey!"

"Now watch what happens when we expose an inferior specimen to danger," continued Zock. At this, a panel slid open to reveal the unfortunate Penfold clamped to the wall with a metal band.

"Good grief! It's Penfold!" exclaimed Dangermouse. "Penfold – you all right?"

"Oh! DM! Thank goodness! Yes I'm ... waaagh! No I'm *not*! Ahh! Ooh! Ahh!"

He shrieked at the sudden appearance of a monster wearing boxing gloves.

"What are you doing to Penfold, you big-eared twit?" called our hero.

"It takes one to know one!" commented Zock. "But – to answer your question – the Botulian Basher is going to relieve your colleague of what I think you call his living daylights!"

"Ah! Oh! Waaagh! Don't let him hit me Chief!" screamed Penfold.

"You fiend!" snarled DM. "If only I could get loose!"

"Ah! said Zock, "you only had to ask!" – and pressing a button, he released the confining straps.

"Oof!" said the White Wonder, nonchalantly falling off the table. "Thanks!"

"Oh no! 'Elp!" screeched Penfold and at this, DM leapt to his defence, fending off the Basher with his feet while he unclasped Penfold's bonds.

"There you are!" he laughed as Penfold fell to the floor. "Nothing to it! Come on!"

As they fled down echoing steely corridors, Zock's voice boomed and echoed from hidden speakers.

"This is Dr Zock. The earthlings have escaped! I want them recaptured immediately ... if not sooner!"

"We'll try down here," panted DM.

They hurtled on their way – but not for long ... Soon they were recaptured.

"Jolly strong grip, that guard!" said DM as they sat in their cell. "Has my ear dekinked yet?"

"Oh crumbs, DM," squealed the hamster. "They've got us!"

"Only as long as the door's locked, Penfold! If only we could reach that electronic door control ..."

"Well," said Penfold, thoughtfully, "we could if we opened the door, chief."

"*Thank* you Penfold! No – if we could shoot something at the buttons, it might work. If only I had something like a ... like a – Penfold, you're a genius! Where did you get that peashooter? – loaded too!"

"PHUT! PHUT!" Dangermouse fired at the buttons, hitting them in sequence – 4, 7, 7, 2, 8, 1, 5. With the last dried pea the door swung silently open.

"Come on!" urged Dangermouse – and they ran down a long corridor.

They had covered a good half-mile when their path was blocked by another towering steel door.

"Drat!" said DM. "Another combination lock, too!" and he stabbed at it with a White finger. 12345 – no! 54321 – no! 52431 – no ... Let's try another ..."

"Er – Chief!" interrupted Penfold. "Oo! Hurry Chief!"

"I'm nearly there!"

"Too late!" screeched the horrified hamster. "*He's here*!"

Dangermouse whipped round to see a savage-fanged, pop-eyed, cruel-clawed, fur-clad monster lumbering at them.

"Oh crumbs, ooh crumbs, ooh crumbs! Can't we make a hole in the door, chief?" cried the assistant and, puce with fear, threw himself at the door. For once he didn't miss – and with a terrible graunching of metal he burst through.

Dangermouse turned and smiled at the monster. "You'll have to excuse him. He's allergic to monsters – 'Bye!"

Another five minutes found our heroes struggling into a pair of space suits.

"Quite a fashionable shade of red. Now, Penfold," smiled DM, "we can just walk out past the guards. If ..."

"*If*? If what, Dangermouse?"

"If we can find a door to walk out of! Now what *I* think – Ah! I'll press this button ... Yes! Er – Penfold! What on earth are you doing?" asked Dangermouse in surprise.

Behind Penfold a door had slid open – and though he was running away from it – he was getting nearer and nearer *to* it!

"Oo! Crumbs, DM! I'm trying to stop myself from being sucked out of the door!" wailed Penfold.

"Nonsense, Penfold," DM laughed lightly. "Only the vacuum of space could cause that to happ ... OOF!"

A giant hand seemed to slam him into the door jamb – and the same force caught Penfold and whisked him into the star-speckled void that lay beyond the door.

"Help! He-e-e-lp!" cried the unfortunate hamster while Dangermouse struggled to peel himself from the wall.

"If I could just break free from this force field Greenback's generating!" he gasped.

"Stop me, DM!" cried Penfold.

He stopped. As he hurtled through space, he had encountered an asteroid going the other way. Like a ball off McEnroe's racket, he shot back towards the still-open door of the ship.

"Wooo! ... ooooo!"

At that moment, Dangermouse finally struggled free and, hanging on to a convenient fire-hose set off in pursuit of his assistant – only to meet him in the doorway. Together they rocketed back into the spacecraft. But as they did so a TV screen buzzed into life and Zock's face shimmered before them.

"You've got to – listen to *me*!" said the strange voice.

"Look, Greenback," snapped DM, "will you take that silly mask off? You've had your joke. Enough's enough!"

"I quite agree!" came the voice. "Goodbye!" The screen went blank.

The floor beneath them suddenly wasn't – and they found themselves falling ... first into the Mark III and then, with it, back towards Earth.

"Er – where we going now, DM?" asked Penfold nervously.

"To the Big Ear Tracking Station before Greenback gets his space ship there!"

"What about the aliens?"

"*Aliens*!" snorted the White Wonder. "Don't be ridiculous Penfold! No, the Baron didn't fool *me*! Look – there's the station – if we'd been captured by aliens and not Greenback, he would have been here and stolen it!"

"Er – DM ... !" broke in Penfold.

"Mmm?"

"Look!"

And there, hanging above them was the Baron's Frog's Head Flyer. A flap below it slid open and a loudspeaker hinged out from which came Greenback's evil voice:

"Welcome to my trap, Dangermouse! So glad you could make it! I had so much difficulty trying to steal the Station, I decided to come back and destroy it. And you with it!" hissed the Toad as a laser gun emerged from his craft. "And since this is goodbye here is your farewell present!"

"In just ten seconds," he went on, "you will be the world's *latest* detective! Hee, hee, hee. 10, 9, 8, 7, 6, 5, 4, 3, 2, 1 ..."

"Goodbye old friend!" whispered DM.

"Oh crumbs!" gulped Penfold as they waited for the fatal "zero".

But it never came – instead they heard a gasp from Greenback and opened their eyes to see a vast space-ship, glittering with lights which hung above – and dwarfed – the Frog's Head Flyer.

As they watched a great tube probed out of the base of the craft and the Baron's ship suddenly disappeared into it.

"Good grief!" gasped DM – as the huge craft lifted slowly away.

Then, booming out across the gap between them, they heard a familiar voice:

"In contrast to our last two specimens, this is a typical fat earth villain –"

"Fat! How dare you!" they heard the Baron hiss angrily.

"Cor!" said Penfold. "They *were* aliens, Dangermouse – they *were* ali . . . DM? You all right?"

Dangermouse, with a strange look on his face, giggled, giggled again . . . and fainted!

"Oh crumbs!" groaned Penfold. "Wake up, DM, please! Oh crumbs – and we've got another adventure to get through yet! Dangermouse, you don't want Colonel K to see you like this . . ."

INVISIBLE INK

Ridiculous, Penfold! You do not use an invisible pen! YOU would always be losing it for a start!

I shall outline a few easy methods – all approved by H.Q.

Eldnac Xaw Method (favoured by Colonel K as he can also use the candles to wax his moustache).

You need a white wax candle – those little ones used for birthday cakes would be excellent.

Remove the wick first, then sharpen the point with a knife being very careful to point it away from you. Ask permission first!

When you write on the paper the message will be invisible. To develop it sprinkle a dusting of powdered coloured chalk over the paper.

The powder should stick to the writing when you shake the surplus off. Powder scrapings of pencil lead will also achieve this. Only don't upset Colonel K by getting into a mess!

Lemon Kurd Method taught to me by nomadic tribesmen during a visit to Kurdistan).

Using a cocktail stick, write the message with lemon juice. It will become invisible as the paper dries.

To read the message your contact simply heats the paper gently over an electric light bulb or candle. (Don't hold the paper too close to the flame.)

Remember, agents, the person to whom you give your message – perhaps included in an otherwise innocent letter – will need to know there *is* a secret message and also what "developer" to use.

Agree a code beforehand. "Cheers from . . ." at the end means a message.

A date written in figures means "use heat".

A date when the month is written as a word means "use powder".

The DANGERMOUSE HIDEOUT

You might think that having a secret agent's H.Q. in a Mayfair pillar-box would have considerable disadvantages – like being buried in football pool coupons every Friday night and finding that half the wall was swinging open three times a day.

This pillar-box, though is different. As you will see, the slot opens into a large pipe which in turn leads to a temporary storage chamber below ground level.

At regular intervals, the stored letters are sucked out and travel along a communicating pipe until they come to rest in a matching pillar-box in Willesden Green.

Try posting a letter to yourself in this pillar-box in Mayfair (security requirements prevent us from telling you *exactly* where it is) and you will find that it will be postmarked 'Willesden Green'.

Far from being cluttered with letters and postcards D.M.'s home is fitted out with all that the World's Greatest Secret Agent might need.

Extensive Reference Library:
Where D. M. keeps detailed maps, criminal records and dictionaries of the world's rarest languages such as Turbo-Stoat, Rirweeli and Barnsleyite. [Because of the H.Q.'s circular shape, there was considerable difficulty in fitting the bookshelves to the wall. This problem was overcome by using planks made from the wood of the banana tree.]

D.M.'s Wardrobe/ Changing Room:
He has 730 identical white suits and 730 black eye-patches which allow for a complete change of clothing every morning and evening.

They are made from a unique synthetic fibre specially developed by D.M. from his No. 3 chemistry set.

This Trihexybutylchloro-mentholhydro-oxylmo-lybelenomdicotyledonous-pollybide is water-proof, thorn-proof, heat-proof, cold-proof, moth-proof, wear-proof, dirt-proof and bullet-proof.

Penfold's Bedroom:

The only bedroom. That is because our hero never sleeps. Penfold, on the other hand, is only properly awake when he is scared. His cot has closely spaced bars to prevent the bogey-man from nibbling his tootsies in the night.

Detachable Escape Module:

For use in the event of flood, fire or earthquake. In flight it looks remarkably like the science-fiction writers' idea of a flying-saucer.

Early testing of the device over Wharbridge generated many reports of UFOs on which, of course, the government could not comment.

Main Living Room:

This will be familiar to all viewers of the Dangermouse series. Simply decorated, it has a semi-circular couch so that people can sit around, and set into the wall is the Mark III Fishuki Videophone.

Central Lift Mechanism:

Any alarm call sets it in a state of readiness. After that it needs only the weight of D.M. leaping onto the couch to activate the high-speed hydraulic mechanism which drops the passengers at 347 grams per square yard into the garage area.

The rapidly descending weight compresses the shock-absorbing fluid into the central column and at 1.37 STTD (seconds to touch down) this pressure is used to power an hydraulic starter motor on D.M.'s car.

At 0.92 STTD the couch reaches the base of the column and a hinge mechanism flips the seating forward thus propelling our heroes into their appropriate seats in the car.

DANGERMOUSE'S CAR

The Mark III car is a masterpiece of automouseic engineering. Watching it turn right-angle corners at high speed, it is clear that its road-holding is of superb quality. It is a very advanced vehicle with some useful features that were not built into the Mark I or II models.

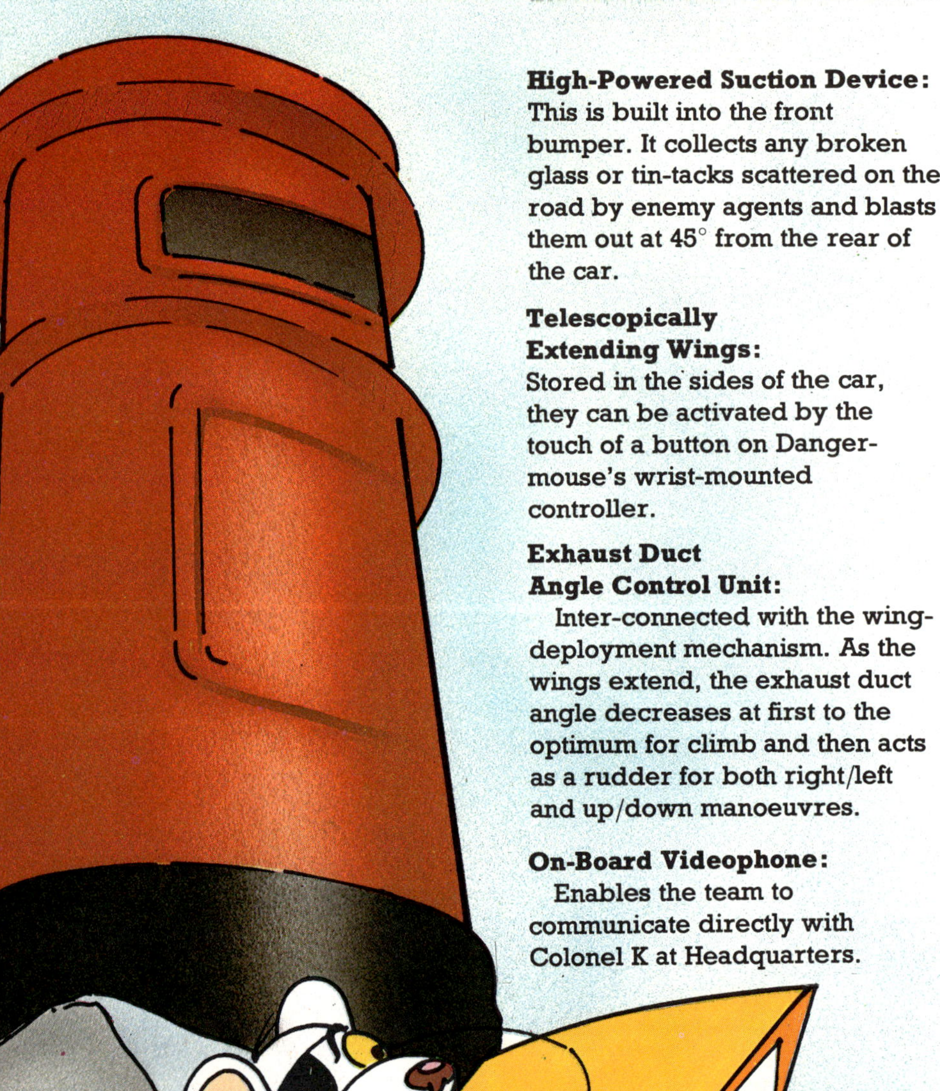

High-Powered Suction Device:
This is built into the front bumper. It collects any broken glass or tin-tacks scattered on the road by enemy agents and blasts them out at 45° from the rear of the car.

Telescopically Extending Wings:
Stored in the sides of the car, they can be activated by the touch of a button on Dangermouse's wrist-mounted controller.

Exhaust Duct Angle Control Unit:
Inter-connected with the wing-deployment mechanism. As the wings extend, the exhaust duct angle decreases at first to the optimum for climb and then acts as a rudder for both right/left and up/down manoeuvres.

On-Board Videophone:
Enables the team to communicate directly with Colonel K at Headquarters.

See-Through Canopy:
3.73% of the airflow through the ducting system is diverted so as to provide a high-speed and impenetrable air-flow which exits from the rear of the bonnet and acts as a see-through canopy for driver and passenger.

Hydraulically Operated Suspension:
This has one or two unusual features – for instance, through a uniquely manoeuverable hinged and extensible ram the wheels can be placed in any place – enabling the car to be driven up walls, trees, across ceilings (or Sealinks) as well as *down* walls, trees and *back* across ceilings (or Sea Lynx) (but not cuff links). (How about golf links?) (Yes, they'd be O.K.) (Can no-one stop this stuff?)

What's more, the ram extends to 120′ thus allowing the driver to get a good view over the vehicles in front should there be a diplodocus jam. (Have you ever *tasted* diplodocus jam? It's disgust . . .) (Don't start that again!) (No – sorry!).

Extending Loud-Speaker Mechanism:
For addressing dangerous criminals who have been surrounded by Dangermouse, terrifying advancing enemy hordes with tapes of Colonel K playing the trombone or, in Penfold's case, shouting for help.

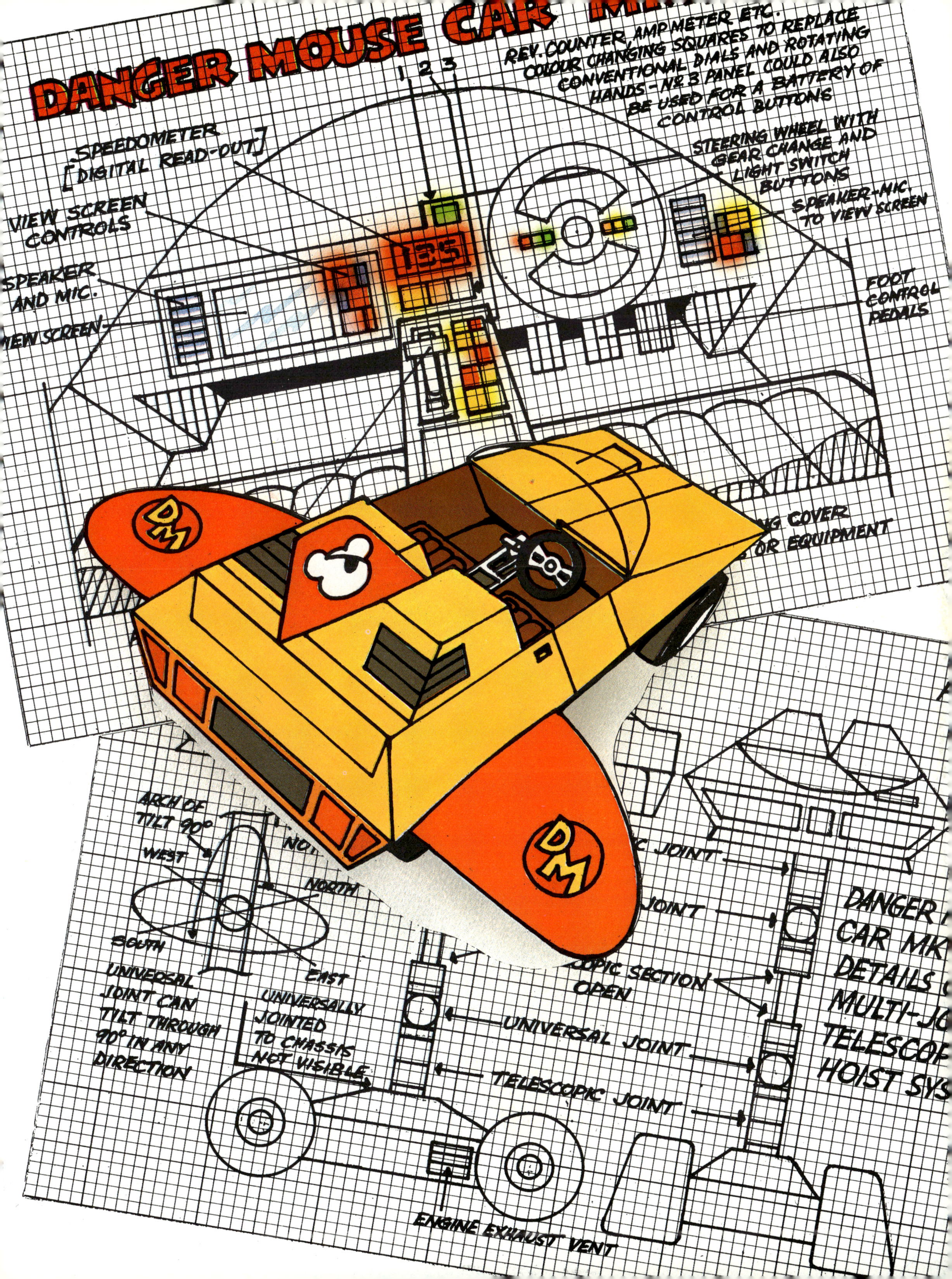

DANGER MOUSE CAR MK
REV. COUNTER, AMP METER ETC. COLOUR CHANGING SQUARES TO REPLACE CONVENTIONAL DIALS AND ROTATING HANDS – № 3 PANEL COULD ALSO BE USED FOR A BATTERY OF CONTROL BUTTONS
1 2 3
SPEEDOMETER [DIGITAL READ-OUT]
STEERING WHEEL WITH GEAR CHANGE AND LIGHT SWITCH BUTTONS
VIEW SCREEN CONTROLS
SPEAKER-MIC. TO VIEW SCREEN
135
SPEAKER AND MIC.
FOOT CONTROL PEDALS
VIEW SCREEN
OR EQUIPMENT
DM
DM
ARCH OF TILT 90°
WEST
NORTH
SOUTH
EAST
UNIVERSAL JOINT CAN TILT THROUGH 90° IN ANY DIRECTION
UNIVERSALLY JOINTED TO CHASSIS NOT VISIBLE
JOINT
JOINT
SECTION OPEN
UNIVERSAL JOINT
TELESCOPIC JOINT
ENGINE EXHAUST VENT

DANGER MOUSE
DAY OF THE SUDS
MAKING THE MOST OF A FEW OFF DUTY MOMENTS DANGERMOUSE AND PENFOLD WERE SORTING THE LAUNDRY WHEN THE VIDEOPHONE ALARM WENT.
GOOD HEAVENS, COLONEL, YOU LOOK AS WHITE AS A SHEET!
AS WELL I MIGHT, DM. LONDON'S BEEN INVADED! WASHING MACHINES! HUNDREDS OF 'EM. BREAKING OUT OF HOUSES, LAUNDERETTES — EVERYWHERE!
SECONDS LATER DANGERMOUSE AND PENFOLD WERE ROARING THROUGH LONDON IN SEARCH OF THE WASHING MACHINES.
AH! AT LAST— A LEAD — SOAP SUDS!
I'M SURE I DIDN'T PUT TOO MUCH POWDER IN!
THE TRAIL OF THE SUDS LED TO A HIGH LEDGE BELOW WHICH THEY COULD SEE THOUSANDS OF WASHING MACHINES. GREENBACK'S VOICE BOOMED OVER A LOUDSPEAKER.
NOW HEAR THIS! YOU WILL OBEY THE VOICE OF TOAD! SEEK AND DESTROY-DANGERMOUSE!
CRUMBS, CHIEF! NOW WHAT DO WE DO?
RUN FOR IT, PENFOLD. THESE MACHINES HAVE BEEN FITTED WITH TOAD VOICE RESPONDER UNITS — THEY'LL DO WHATEVER GREENBACK COMMANDS.
CRUMBS, DM, THAT WAS A NARROW SQUEAK!
LUCKY THEY DON'T HAVE WINGS. THERE'S A WHOLE ARMY OF THE BLESSED THINGS AND WE MIGHT NOT GET A SECOND CHANCE...
IT'LL BE A FIGHT TO THE DEATH — I CAN'T SEE THEM SURRENDERING.
OH — NO NEED FOR THAT — I'LL SURRENDER — EH?
THEY LANDED IN A SCRAP YARD AND HID IN THE CAB OF A CRANE.
NEED TO THINK OF A PLAN. I'M GOING INTO A SEVENTH LEVEL YOGA HOPPING TRANCE. KEEP A LOOK OUT!
OH, FIDDLE! SEVENTH LEVEL! HE COULD BE HOPPING ABOUT FOR DAYS.
PENFOLD, YOU'VE SWITCHED ON THE GIANT MAGNET! RIGHT LET THE CAR DOWN NICE AND EASY, PENFOLD ... PENFOLD!
OH, ECK! WHAT 'AVE I DONE. I DIDN'T MEAN TO SWITCH IT ON, SIR.

OH, CRUMBS! CHIEF! CHIEF! ARE YOU ALRIGHT?
I'M JUST GLAD IT'S A REAR ENGINED CAR, PENFOLD. NOW, I MUST CONTACT THE COLONEL....
WHILE SQUADRONS OF AIRBORNE MACHINES ADVANCED DANGERMOUSE CALMLY MADE PLANS....
WELL, I DON'T KNOW, DM – YOU REALLY SEEM TO THINK I CAN MOVE HEAVEN AND EARTH...
CHIEF, LOOK!
LOOK, SIR, OUR FUTURES DEPEND ON IT AND... SORRY, SIR, GOT TO DASH.
THE SKY WAS AWASH WITH MACHINES.
WHA-WHA-WHATEVER ARE THEY? OOO!
KAMIKAZE TWINTUBS, PENFOLD! TIME TO MOVE!
THE INTREPID PAIR MADE THEIR GETAWAY WITH MACHINES CRASHING ALL AROUND THEM
WHY KAMIKAZE?
THEY ALL COMMIT SUISUDS AT THE END OF THE RINSE CYCLE.
FAILED! THEY ESCAPED! STILETTO! LIQUIDATE!
SI, BARONE!
BANG! WHOOSH BUBBLE BUBBLE!
MEANWHILE DANGERMOUSE IS PUTTING HIS PLUCKY PLAN INTO OPERATION.
BY JOVE HE'S DONE IT! THE COLONEL'S DONE IT!
DONE WHAT, CHIEF? AND WHAT'S THAT BIG HOLE FOR?
IT'S AN IRRESISTIBLE INVITATION TO ALL THOSE WASHING MACHINES. LOOK, PENFOLD, HERE THEY COME!

OUT OF CONTROL! OUT OF CONTROL!
SWITCH OFF MAGNET... NOW!
SOON DANGERMOUSE'S PIT WAS PILED HIGH WITH MACHINES.
COME BACK! UNGRATEFUL MACHINES! STILETTO! DESTROY THEM ALL!
SI, BARONE.
BUT, LIKE A PHOENIX RISING FROM THE ASHES, FROM OUT OF THE SOAP SUDS AROSE...
GOOD GRIEF! A HIDEOUS MUTATED MONSTER! HURRY PENFOLD!
AAAGH! CRIKEY!
I SUPPOSE HE THINKS THAT'S FUNNY! AND STOP FOAMING AT THE MOUTH! PENFOLD, RUN!
YE-ES, SIR!
BACK IN THE CAR THEY SCOUR THE SOAKING CITY FOR THE FOAM-FILLED FURY
HIDING BEHIND A SKYSCRAPER, I DARE SAY! LET'S TAKE A LOOK, PENFOLD.
WAAAGH! DANGERMOUSE, HELP!
IN HOT PURSUIT OF THE MONSTER AND PENFOLD DANGERMOUSE ARRIVES AT TRAFALGAR SQUARE.
NELSON? LYING DOWN? HE USED TO HAVE A REALLY TOP JOB IN TRAFALGAR... GOOD GRIEF! IT'S UP THERE!
RIGHT, YOU FOAMING FIEND! HERE I COME!
IT'S NO USE, DM! HE'LL PULVERISE YOU!

LOOK- IF YOU GIVE UP NOW- ER- I WON'T LET HIM HIT YOU! OO-ER!
GOOD GRIEF!
BUT DANGERMOUSE GUESSED THE MONSTER'S WEAK SPOT...
HA! HA! HA!
TICKLE-WICKLE! THIS LITTLE PIGGY....
HA! HA! HA! TEE HEE HEE!
AAAAGH! HEEEELP!
PENFOLD! WELCOME BACK!
HA! HA! AAAGH!
WELL, WELL. JUST AS I THOUGHT!
WHAT, CHIEF?
THE KINETIC FORCES HAVE IONISED THE ELECTRO-CHEMICAL BOND WITH RESULTANT REVERSION!
COR! GREAT! ER- WHAT'S THAT MEAN?
HIS BUBBLE'S BURST, PENFOLD. HE'S GONE BACK TO WHAT HE WAS MADE FROM — SOAP SUDS!
CRUMBS- ER, OR RATHER- SUDS!

DISGUISES

There are many different ways to disguise yourself – make-up, clothes, changing your build or age, and – very important indeed – changing your usual habits and general behaviour.

Of course, the most famous Master of Disguise is our own Agent 57 – renowned for his cunning costumes which can transform him from worm to polar bear or anything else he likes.

In fact no-one really knows what he looks like! I have asked him along – at least I think it's him, you can never be sure – to give you a few tips.

Before we start on make-up, which is rather expensive unless you have a sympathetic mother or big sister, remember there are simpler things.

Hair: the way the hair is arranged or parted can make a surprising difference, while a pair of sun glasses makes recognition even more difficult.

What's that, Penfold – You've just walked into a chair! Half-witted hamster, I told you not to buy glasses that were too dark.

EYEBROWS are the easiest to alter, your own being "whitened out" first by using white soap which you then allow to dry. With the eyebrow pencil then draw in different shaped brows, angling them to give the expression you need.

Or, without the soap, you may darken your own brows and make them heavier.

EYES may be "altered" by use of shadow and wrinkles, taking care not to get anything in the eye itself. Softly, softly does it!

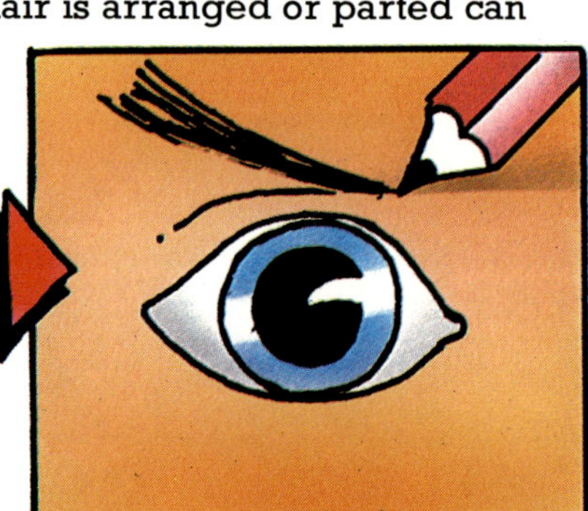

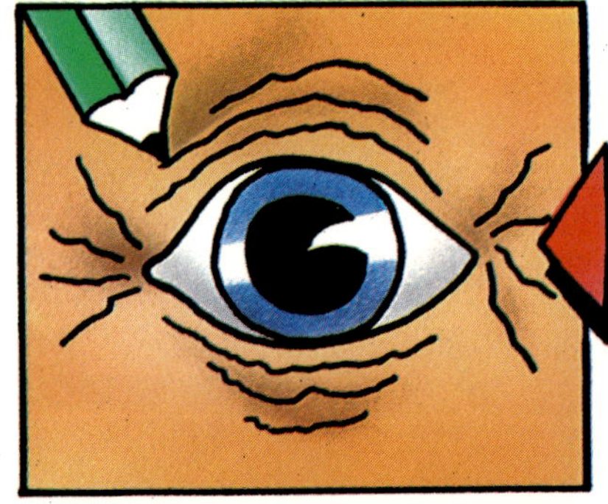

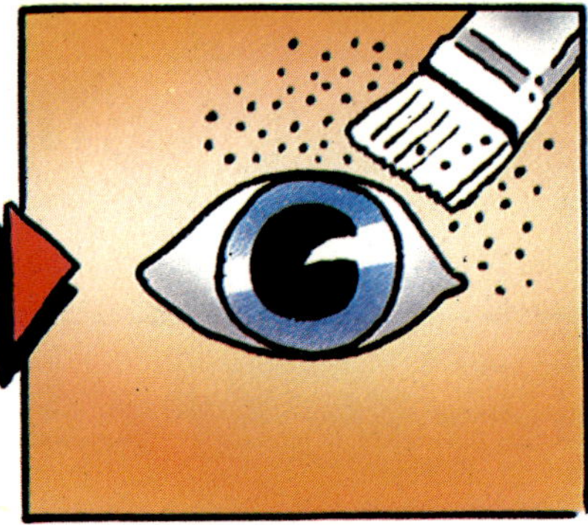

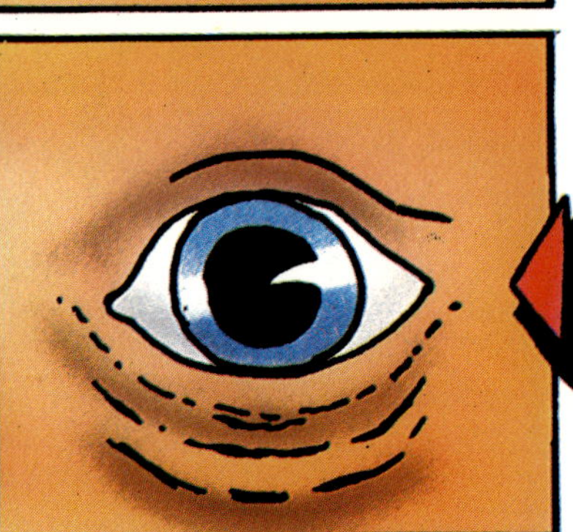

Light use of the pencil provides wrinkles, to make you look older or "laughter" lines.

Powdering around the eyes with eye-shadow can make them brighter; heavier shadow gives a more sunken appearance.

Lines beneath the eyes can be shaded for a "baggy" effect, particularly to suggest old age – or old Greenback himself.

Now for SPECIAL EFFECTS! No, not like when Penfold disguised himself as a PILLAR BOX – and very well too – because it fooled me into posting a letter. Just as well it was written on rice paper!

No, I'm thinking of things like scars, missing teeth, eye patches and bandages. All very useful additions.

Missing teeth can be suggested by blacking out real ones by means of tiny squares of black paper stuck on with a smear of treacle. Never use glue or anything in tubes!

Huge teeth can be suggested by cutting them from orange peel, slipping the section into your mouth (white side outwards).

Scars are drawn with a sliver of lipstick.

Moustaches can very easily be drawn on using a burnt cork. Simply hold a cork in the flame of a candle (making sure your fingers are well out of the way!) Turn it until the end is blackened. You can then use it like a pencil to draw moustaches and beards. Be careful! If you touch your moustache it will smudge – a tell-tale sign to your enemies.

CHANGING YOUR BUILD: It's very hard to make yourself thinner but "bulking up" is a real piece of cake. "Ha Ha! That's very funny!" Penfold will you control yourself! To seem fat you just tie a cushion or cushions around your waist (back and front) and wear an overcoat over them. Scarves around legs and arms can bulk out your trousers and sleeves to complete the effect.

Once "fatter", you need to waddle a little, wear a scarf to conceal your neck and turn up your collar.

A hat and glasses are useful, for these will help you to **LOOK OLD**. Stoop, use a stick, let a little white wool stick out from under your hat. Act old, but keep your wits sharp. If you drop something remember not to pick it up like a flash. Moving slowly gives you time to look around, watch for enemies and gain information without being conspicuous.

Bubblegum in the cheeks can alter facial expressions and is far more pleasant than wax or cottonwool. But don't make yourself look like a hamster, for this upsets Penfold.

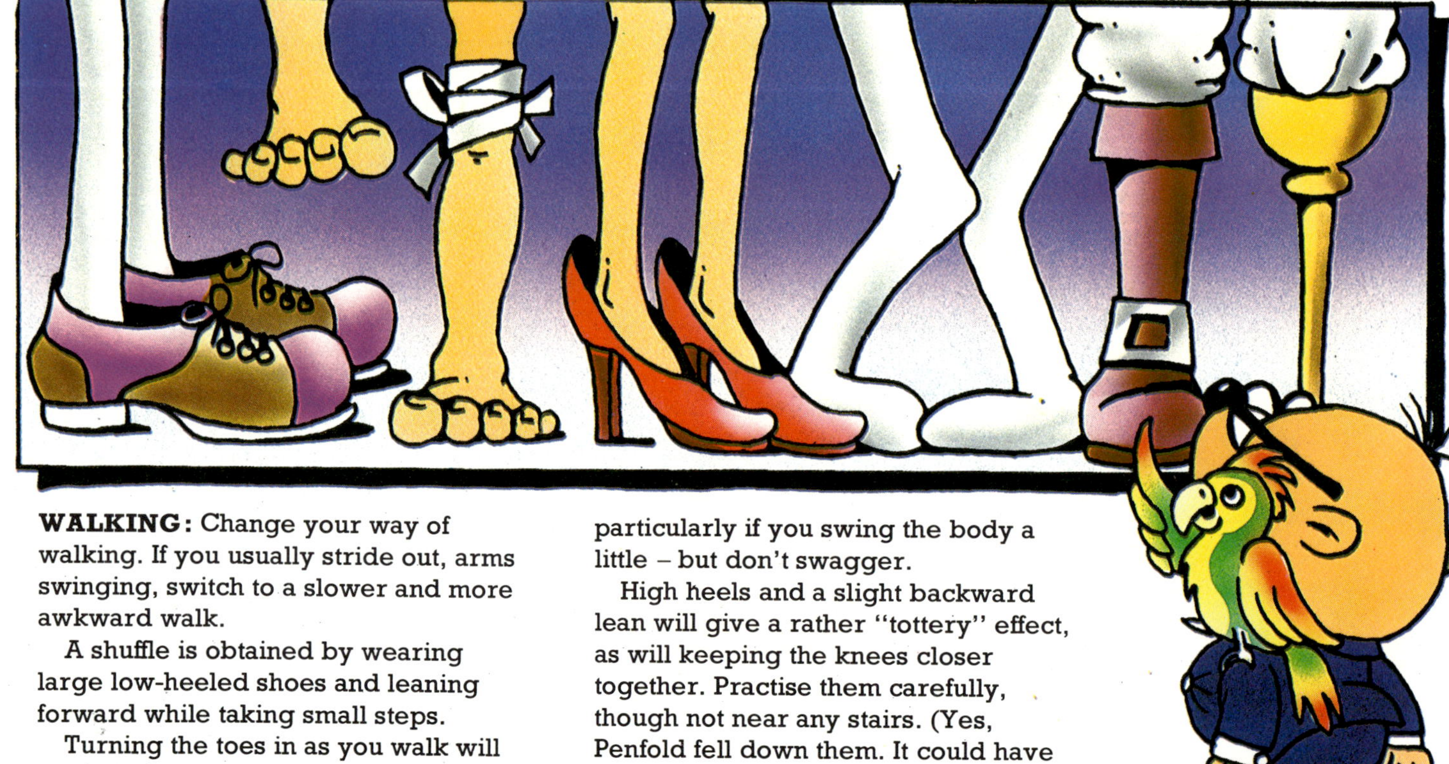

WALKING: Change your way of walking. If you usually stride out, arms swinging, switch to a slower and more awkward walk.

A shuffle is obtained by wearing large low-heeled shoes and leaning forward while taking small steps.

Turning the toes in as you walk will again make you move very differently, particularly if you swing the body a little – but don't swagger.

High heels and a slight backward lean will give a rather "tottery" effect, as will keeping the knees closer together. Practise them carefully, though not near any stairs. (Yes, Penfold fell down them. It could have been worse – it might have been ME!)

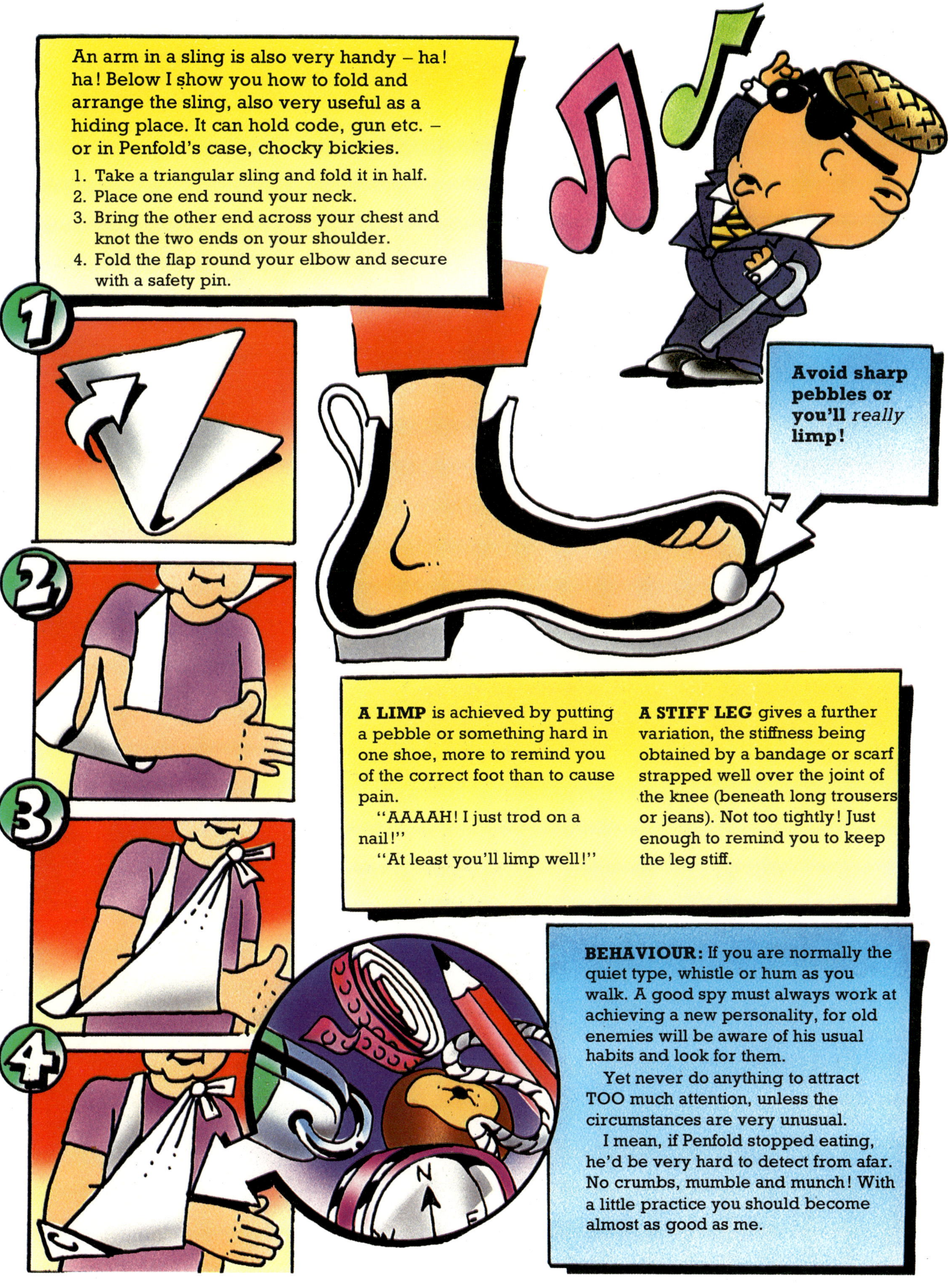

An arm in a sling is also very handy – ha! ha! Below I show you how to fold and arrange the sling, also very useful as a hiding place. It can hold code, gun etc. – or in Penfold's case, chocky bickies.

1. Take a triangular sling and fold it in half.
2. Place one end round your neck.
3. Bring the other end across your chest and knot the two ends on your shoulder.
4. Fold the flap round your elbow and secure with a safety pin.

A LIMP is achieved by putting a pebble or something hard in one shoe, more to remind you of the correct foot than to cause pain.

"AAAAH! I just trod on a nail!"

"At least you'll limp well!"

A STIFF LEG gives a further variation, the stiffness being obtained by a bandage or scarf strapped well over the joint of the knee (beneath long trousers or jeans). Not too tightly! Just enough to remind you to keep the leg stiff.

BEHAVIOUR: If you are normally the quiet type, whistle or hum as you walk. A good spy must always work at achieving a new personality, for old enemies will be aware of his usual habits and look for them.

Yet never do anything to attract TOO much attention, unless the circumstances are very unusual.

I mean, if Penfold stopped eating, he'd be very hard to detect from afar. No crumbs, mumble and munch! With a little practice you should become almost as good as me.

SPOT the SPIES

This busy station is not all that it seems! Can you spot the spies?
There are also 7 items of spy equipment hidden in the picture. Can you find them?

There's only one Greenback .. or is there? We seem to have a few imposters here – or is this another of the evil toad's devious schemes? Which is the *real* Greenback?

Answers on page 78

DANGER MOUSE
ICE STATION CAMEL
DANGERMOUSE AND HIS TRUSTY ASSISTANT, PENFOLD WERE RETURNING FROM YET ANOTHER SUCCESSFUL MISSION.
WHAT ARE YOU GOING TO DO WITH IT, DANGERMOUSE?
I DON'T KNOW, HONESTLY, WHEN THEY SAID THEY WANTED TO GIVE ME SOMETHING, I WAS HOPING IT WOULD BE A MEDAL, NOT A BLOOMIN' GREAT TEDDY BEAR!
HE'LL HAVE TO STAY IN THE ZOO WITH MY ELEPHANT
AND YOUR TIGER, YOUR THREE-TOED SLOTH, YOUR MONGOLIAN WILD MULE..
COLONEL K APPEARED ON THE T.V. SCREEN
CALLING AGENT DANGERMOUSE. ARE YOU THERE?
YES, COLONEL. IF I WASN'T, I'D BE SOMEWHERE ELSE, NOW WOULDN'T I?
NOT ANOTHER ANIMAL GIFT, D.M.? THEY ALWAYS MAKE YOU TETCHY. GOT A BIT OF A PROBLEM — MORE OF A CATASTROPHE. THE WORLD'S STOPPING.
CRUMBS!
GOOD GRIEF! WE'D BETTER GET MOVING THEN, SIR — AS SOON AS WE'VE DROPPED FRED AT THE ZOO!
MEANWHILE, FAR AWAY IN THE FROZEN NORTH, THAT AMBITIOUS AMPHIBIAN, BARON GREENBACK WAS TRYING TO CHANGE THE LAW OF GRAVITY.
MY ANTI-GRAVITY ROTATION RETARDER ATTACHED TO THE NORTH POLE WILL BRING THE WORLD TO A HALT AND SMALL OBJECTS WILL START FALLING OFF! THEN I SHALL SPEAK TO THE WORLD AS THE ONLY ONE WITH THE POWER TO SAVE IT!
TEE HEE HEE!
BUT WHAT IF THEY WON'T LISTEN, BARONE?
THEY WILL BE FLUNG INTO OUTER SPACE! THE ALARM! THERE'S SOMETHING NEAR THE MACHINE! STILETTO, FIRE!
A POLAR BEAR SNIFFING ROUND THE MACHINE SUDDENLY LEAPT AWAY AS STILETTO HIT IT
YOU DOLT, STILETTO! YOU BARELY GRAZED IT!
VERY FUNNY, BARONE - BEARLY! VERY GOOD!
TEE HEE HEE

FOLLOWING A HUNCH – OR MAYBE IT'S A HUSKY – DANGERMOUSE WAS HEADING FOR THE NORTH POLE.
NOT LONG NOW, PENFOLD. ABOUT AN HOUR AS THE CROW FLIES.
WHY WOULD A CROW WANT TO GO TO THE NORTHPOLE?
FOR THE SNOWBALL FIGHTS, OF COURSE.
AT THE NORTH POLE DANGERMOUSE AND PENFOLD EXAMINE GREENBACK'S MACHINE.
IT'S AN ANTI-GRAVITY ROTATION RETARDER – A SET OF BRAKES! THIS THING IS SLOWING THE WORLD DOWN.
CRIKEY! OH ECK! WHAT ARE WE GOING TO DO?
DANGERMOUSE PRESSED A BUTTON.
I THINK THIS SHOULD STOP.. ..AAAGH!
CRUMBS! WHAT HAPPENED?
HE FELL DOWN THAT HOLE.
I KNOW THAT. I MEAN.. ..OH! WHO ARE YOU? AAAGH! HELP! BYE!
DANGERMOUSE FOUND HIMSELF FACING THE EVIL BARON GREENBACK.
TUT, TUT. YOU DIDN'T REALLY THINK IT WOULD BE THAT EASY TO STOP, DID YOU, DANGERMOUSE?
I'M NOT THE FOOL YOU THINK I AM, GREENBACK! I KNEW IF I TAMPERED WITH THE MACHINE IT'S OWNER WOULD SHOW HIMSELF. YOU'RE UNDER ARREST.
BUT GREENBACK WASN'T BEATEN YET. HE PRESSED A BUTTON AND DANGERMOUSE ROCKETED SKYWARDS.
PERHAPS THEY'LL APPRECIATE HIM MORE ON THE MOON! HA, HA, HA! I'M RID OF HIM AT LAST!
POOR PENFOLD WAS FAR FROM HAPPY
I DON'T KNOW, IT'S ALRIGHT FOR HIM. HE DOESN'T FEEL THE COLD LIKE I DO. THEN HE GOES SWANNING OFF, HAVING ALL THE FUN, LEAVING ME TO BE EATENBY A POLAR BEAR.
JUST THEN DANGERMOUSE ZOOMED PAST.
BE WITH YOU IN A MINUTE, PENFOLD.
RIGHT, DM..! WAIT A MINUTE! WHAT ABOUT ME?

PENFOLD TURNED TO SEE THE BEAR
NOW I'M WARNING YOU! I'M A MASTER OF THE DEADLY ART OF KUNG MOGGIE! YOU'RE NOT GOING TO EAT ME!
EAT YOU! WHAT A HORRIBLE THOUGHT! DON'T YOU KNOW POLAR BEARS ONLY EAT MINTS?
I'M NOT REALLY A BEAR ANYWAY. I'M AGENT 57.
THE MASTER OF DISGUISE! GOOD GRIEF!
SUDDENLY THE MACHINE EXPLODED! PENFOLD FOUND HIMSELF STANDING ON THE EDGE OF A GAPING HOLE.
OH! CRUMBS! IT WASN'T ME! I DIDN'T TOUCH ANYTHING!
CHINS UP, PENFOLD. THAT'S ANOTHER SUCCESSFUL MISSION OVER.
NORTH POLE
DANGERMOUSE! BUT HOW DID YOU.... I MEAN WHERE DID YOU....
SIMPLE, PENFOLD. WHEN I SHOT OUT OF THAT HOLE I BUMPED INTO BUGGLES PIGEON - REMEMBER HIM? HELPED US ON THE GIANT CHICKEN CASE. HE FLEW ME TO THE SOUTH POLE. THERE I QUICKLY CONSTRUCTED A DEVICE FROM MY WATCH THAT WOULD SPEED THE WORLD UP. IT PUT A STRAIN ON GREENBACK'S MACHINE, CAUSING IT TO EXPLODE.
BY THE WAY, PENFOLD, WHERE'S GREENBACK?
DOWN THERE - UNDERNEATH AGENT 57
THEIR MISSION SUCCESSFULLY COMPLETED THE DYNAMIC DUO RETURNED TO BASE
NICE OF THOSE ESKIMOS TO HELP US GET GREENBACK OUT OF THAT HOLE AND OFF TO JAIL.
BUT ESKIMOS DON'T HAVE MEDALS
I DIDN'T THINK THEY HAD CAMELS, EITHER. HE IS RATHER NICE, THOUGH, ISN'T HE?
I SUPPOSE HE IS, IN A LUMPY KIND OF WAY.

MAKE A DANGERMOUSE MASK

Trace the mask onto a piece of card. Cut it out and colour it. Cut a hole for the eye. Make a hole on either side and thread thin elastic through. Now you can *really* be a superspy!

SPY RING

Penfold is getting all excited now. Pardon me while I explain to him. We are not, I repeat NOT, talking of doughnut rings, Penfold. Ah, he understands. He gasped "Crikey!"

We are talking, Penfold, of a unit or group of spies – each group being known as a ring. Different members play different parts, each member has his own code-name.

You give each of your friends his code-name – the names of trees are easy to remember. Elm, Ash, Birch, Oak and so on. No, Penfold! It has nothing to do with "being up gum trees" at all.

Now, your ring will need: A master spy, director of all the group and its operations, namely THE DIRECTOR. He controls everything and his word is law.

Rather like our own Colonel K, working under the secret code name of Special "K". The fewer who really know him, the better. Only your Top Spies should be in close contact.

For this reason we use CUT-OUTS to act as the go-betweens, carrying the orders and messages between the Director and his spies.

They check on efficiency and trustworthiness of the agents, invaluable in helping the Director to select the best spy for each job.

THE SPIES are the ones who tail enemies, gather secret information and actually carry out the various missions.

It is safer for each spy to know as little as possible about other spies and the whole organisation (Penfold certainly knows very little). Should he then be captured, there is less for him to give away.

PASSWORDS AND CHECKS

Since Cut-Outs need to contact their spies, a quick means of safe identification is needed. Something innocent and undamaging, should the wrong person be approached. You need a password and a reply.

The Cut-Out may ask, "Do you know the time of the Number 6 Bus? Does it stop here?"

The correct reply, for identification, will be: "I'm only sure about No. 7. That never stops.

The answer is one that only the genuine contact is likely to give.

The spy (contact) also generally part-identifies himself by waiting at a particular spot, often carrying a folded newspaper in a pre-arranged manner.

Additional means of recognition may be a pin concealed beneath the jacket lapel, the lapel then pulled back by its owner as if accidentally.

Correct identification can also be made in another way. The Cut-Out tears a playing-card in half and gives a half to each agent.

When the two agents meet, they check their halves – and should have two parts joining neatly together.

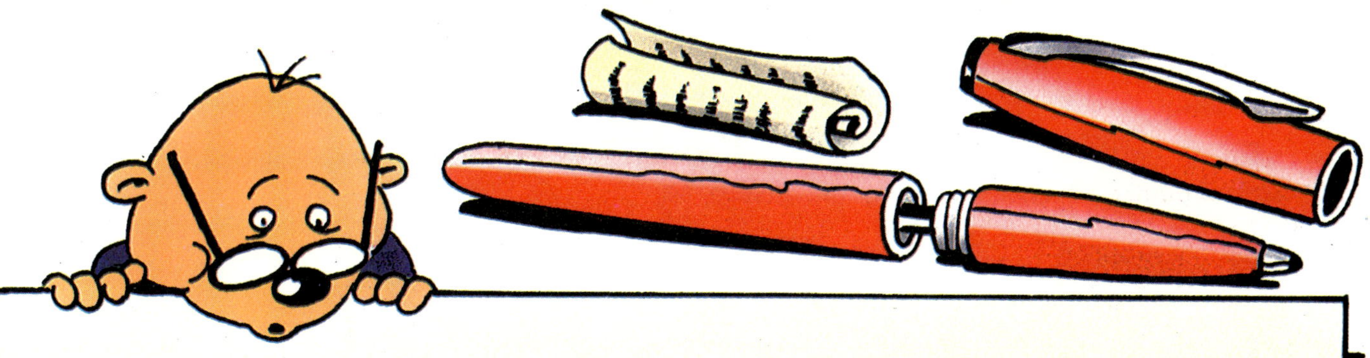

HIDE SECRET MESSAGES

Not in your mouth, nor hand! Roll them up small enough to go inside a ballpoint. Thin paper with small writing can be rolled tightly around the ink tube of the pen.

The lining of your tie is another gimmick. Or within a chocolate bar wrapping. A safe way of passing messages on to your contact.

Trouble is, loss of chocolate. (Very nasty, says Penfold.) You could put a piece of cardboard in an empty chocolate wrapper instead.

You could stick a small message to the back of your belt with selotape. Or sew a secret pocket onto the *inside* of your jeans.

A very thin-nibbed pen is vital for such notes. Also thin paper. Use your own super-cunning to invent similar hiding-places to the examples.

MICRODOTTERY PLOTTERY

Real spies photograph their messages and then reduce the photo (negative) until it is a tiny speck – a MICRODOT. It is so small and innocent that it can be included in a typed letter as a full stop.

The spy receiving it then "blows up" the microdot until the whole message is readable.

Of course you can't do all that! But you can write very small, using a magnifying glass.

An ordinary letter becomes something very different if the ENVELOPE really holds the punch line. The inner letter is nothing. The tiny message is written on that part of the envelope to be covered by a stamp.

The receiver just steams off the stamps. So simple! Steam from a kettle does the trick. Only don't write in ink that will run.

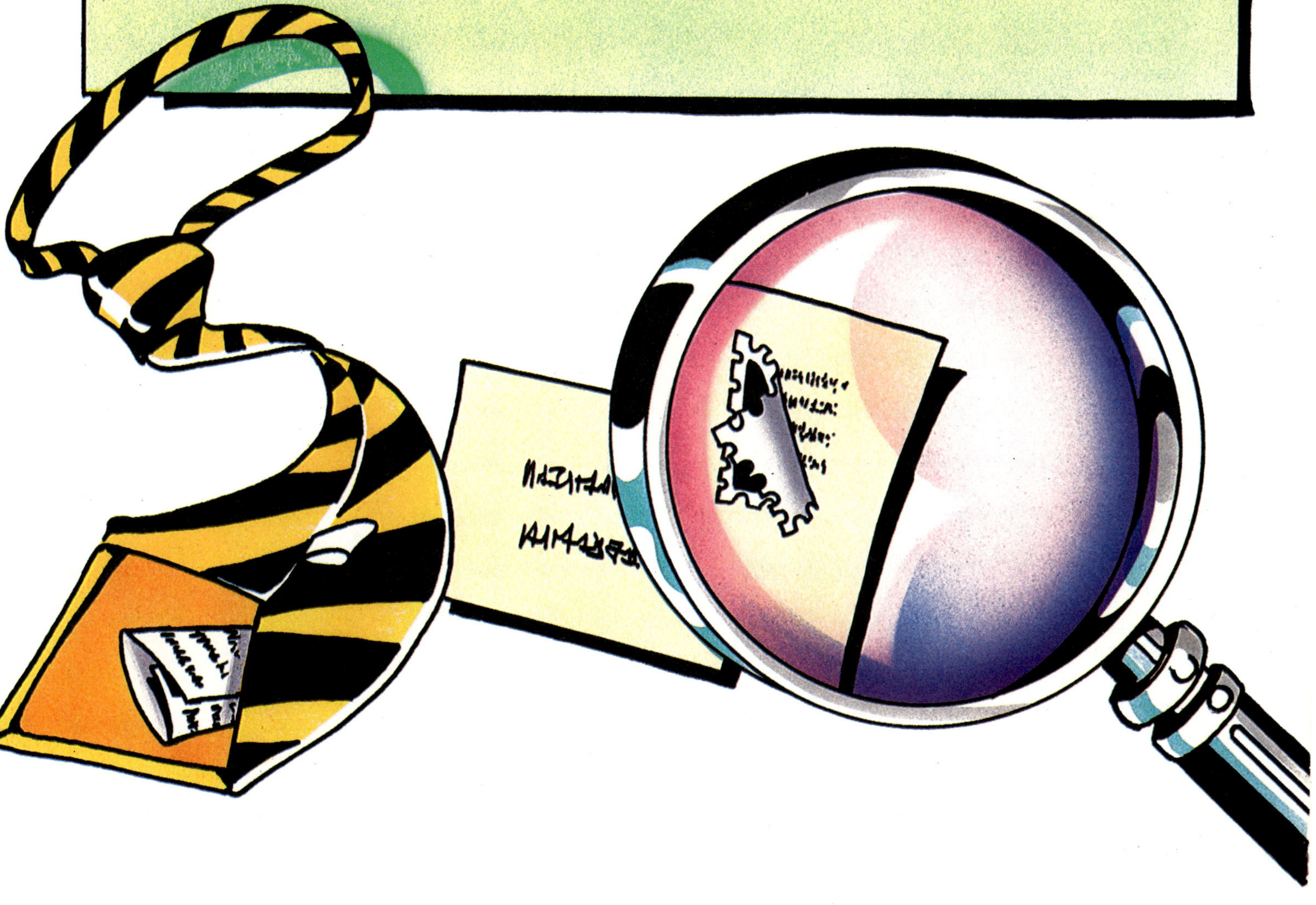

Emergency Signals
Hand across mouth: "Go to HQ!"
Finger on ear: "Wait! Temporary danger!"
Finger across nose: "I have a message!"
Hand across mouth and nose: "Follow me!"
Sending Secret Messages
You can use the Drop or Dead Letter-box – a previously agreed hiding-place. It can be behind a loose brick in a wall or inside a hollow tree.
If you feel it is safe to meet your fellow agent try the Switch. Both agents must carry identical items – ballpoint pens are a good idea.
One agent drops his "accidentally". The second agent helpfully picks it up and apparently hands it back.
But the returned pen is actually a duplicate so the message has changed hands without arousing any suspicion.
In crowded shopping centres you can exchange messages in identical carrier bags. Sit down on a bench next to your contact and pick up the other bag when you leave.
The Switch
Field Telephone
Make a hole in the bottom of 2 empty cans and join them with a length of string. Keep the string taut and you have a telephone!

MAKING CONTACT

The "Meet"

Sometimes messages won't do. You just have to talk to your contact. Obviously risks are involved – you might be overhead by enemy agents – so meetings are for emergencies, like when Penfold ate his rice paper instructions without reading them first.

Choosing the best place is vital. Make it natural – such as feeding ducks in the park. Stroll along the pond scattering bits of your sandwiches. What could be more natural than someone stopping to watch and exchange a few words?

The brief, vital instructions are passed and your contact saunters on. Unless there's a "bug" in a floating decoy duck you have nothing to fear.

MONSTROUS MACHINES

Frog's Head Flyer

An example of Greenback's egotism, the FHF closely resembles its owner in its upper surfaces – though the pedal extremities are somewhat idiosyncratic. (Or, to use Penfold's words, 'it's got funny feet!')

The feet are used to provide a high lift-off speed and a low-velocity touch-down. They also have built in buoyancy – though the proving trials mostly proved that this was a disadvantage.

Stiletto had loaded $4\frac{1}{4}$ tons of spaghetti into the upper dome which caused the craft to adopt a Stable Two position (i.e. upside down). The floating feet then made it impossible to right the FHF.

The three-man (well, two-man and a caterpillar) (well, one toad, one crow and a caterpillar, actually) crew were only saved when Greenback persuaded Stiletto to drink the contents of the Lower Bumbling village pond which had been chosen as the test site.

Stiletto is also responsible for providing the motive power which comes from a large radial fan providing downward thrust to propel the FHF upwards.

The fan, in turn, is powered by the uncoiling of a powerful elastic band (catapult rubber, Grade I) pre-wound by a specially adapted bicycle.

On one occasion the ratchet mechanism slipped during the winding operation and, apart from demolishing a three-foot thick granite wall, Stiletto achieved a new world cycle record by covering $1\frac{1}{2}$ miles in 55 seconds from a standing start.

Big Tom

Big Tom is the product of an evil genius, obsessed with anti-mouse visions, and is the very latest in robotronics. With its six heavily armed arms, it is equipped to nip, snip or flip; to bash, crash and squash; to slice, dice and mangle any mouse its computerised video/olfactory detectors detect.

$2\frac{1}{2}$ Ton Pincers:
These can just as easily restrain D.M. by the end of his nose as they can crush the Mark III to the size of a tin of sardines. (Note that should it be required to do both these operations at once, there is a matching pincer on the upper right arm.)

Electro-Magnetic Fist:
This can be set in either of two modes: (a) to attract any metal elements – such as the Mark III car or the adjusters on Penfold's braces (b) to repel any metal constructed weapons, missiles or other devices.

Giant Pastry Wheel:
Edges and points are sharpened to 9.7 on the Pynch–Chopham scale. In its fixed position it can either jab or slice – but it can also revolve at up to 250 r.p.m.

Modified Spherical Headache Pill:
Drop-forged out of 18/80 stainless steel, the surface of the sphere is furnished with hollow hemispheres which are filled with deadly curare poison.

In this way, a 525 m.p.h. blow on the head from the $2\frac{1}{2}$ hundred-weight sphere is almost always fatal.

Variable Angle Weight-Reducer:
Ultra-sharp, it will slice a single mouse-hair in two should a gentle draught waft it against its edge.

Especially useful in discouraging law-enforcement officers from asking awkward questions.

Hot-Lips Oral Flame-Thrower:
A high-pressure oxy-catty gas flame is projected through a ceramic nozzle when the mechanical jaws are in the 'open' mode at temperatures in excess of 1800°C.

In the end the Hot-Lips Oral Flame-Thrower turned out to be the downfall of Big Tom.

The flame-thrower's direction was controlled manually by Stiletto Mafiosa. Dangermouse fans will recall that he was attempting to produce barbecued D.M., as our hero leapt to and fro on the upper portion of Big Tom's body, while the pincers aimed to grab him.

D.M.'s reactions, however, were so fast that the pincers closed on the flame-thrower, bottling up the high temperature gases and causing the total destruction of yet another evil device.

Polar Rotation Retarding Revolvers

Generally accepted as the most ingeniously evil device ever concocted by Baron Silas Greenback. Transported to the North Pole by a fleet of Camels clad in thermal underwear, it was assembled under the supervision of Nero (the only one with 'O' level maths).

The aim was to apply a contra-rotating force to the North Pole if the world powers failed to accede to the Baron's demands.

The result of this awesome event would have been to catapult every building, animal, vegetable, human or inhuman being into space – and the nearer the Equator, the faster.

The two high-friction rollers are kept in contact with the pole by spring-loaded pinions working on off-set trunnions located with countersunk bunions and lubricated by onions.

The clue to what is perhaps the most ingenious aspect of the device is what many have believed to be cooling fins, projecting like the teeth of vast combs on either side of the drive casing.

Any serious student of 'Dangermouse', civil engineering or Javanese flower arranging will know that this could not be!

They are, in fact, the entrance tunnels for the propulsion units – the 528,000 gerbils who power the rollers by running on them.

Cynics have queried this gerbil-power and have asked why they should choose to run round in circles. At 38°C below freezing how would *you* keep warm?!

Monstrous Machines

The Baron's Patent Boot-Boy

Designed to stamp out resistance underfoot and to put the boot in, this weapon gave Greenback quite a kick out of life.

There were some early developmental problems – for instance, the Baron and Stiletto visited no less than 728 Army Surplus Stores before they could find a sufficiently large pair of boots.

There was also a near fatal disaster when a lace broke during a trial run causing one boot to detach itself so that the machine performed a 25 mile route march in a 17 foot circle.

Control Accommodation Module:

A perfect sphere is used to achieve the highest possible strength/weight ratio. Its parts were turned on an Eikmeyer Oval Hat Lathe.

All joints are made with a Jamison Crimping Machine and finished on a standard contra-acting beet grater.

Photo-Objective Cathode Ray Transmitter/Relayer:

Provides forward vision.

Müller Biotronic Differential Elbow Joints:

The prototype was fitted with these at the knees, with the result that the device kicked itself in the antenna. Later versions were free of this problem.

For a while, the weapon threatened to extinguish the whole of civilisation – except the boot polish manufacturers.

However, with typical brilliance, Dangermouse realised the militaristic nature of the boots and rightly predicted that they would always obey orders.

Using the extending public address system on the Mark III he commanded the boots to march into the river where they sank without trace.

DANGER MOUSE SAVES THE WORLD AGAIN

It was a cloudless April day – but calm as it looked all was not well.

London, the mighty magnificent metrollops, teetered on the brink of destruction. Chaos stalked the streets with its henchman, Terror – and the call went out to the last hope for civilization – to the hero of so many victories over the powers of Darkness – to the World's Greatest Secret Agent – Dangermouse and his faithful assistant, Penfold!

In their Mayfair pillar-box, the great Mouse was relaxing over a book of Russian quadratic equations while the timid hamster did his muscle-building exercises.

Suddenly the videophone screen jazzed into life with its warning "bleep, bleep!"

"Penfold! I'll bet that's Colonel K to tell us that Chaos stalks the streets with its henchman, Terror!" said Dangermouse.

Colonel K appeared looking worried.

"Ah! D.M.! Good show!" he barked. "Look here – Chaos is stalking the streets with its henchman – Terror!"

"And you want us to save the world, sir?" Dangermouse smiled confidently.

"Here's the problem D.M.!" explained K. "Got this over the satellite network from our old enemy – Baron Silas Greenback!"

He pressed a button and the News in Welsh appeared. Grumbling he tried another, watched a few moments of Dallas but finally succeeded in running the sinister message that Baron Silas Greenback had broadcast to the nations.

"Greetings World!" hissed the Terrible Toad. "You'll be amazed at my genius – or else! Now watch carefully – your lives depend on it!"

The picture changed to a signpost which read "Willesden Green – 4,023 miles".

"Behold," he whispered. A signpost in a remote inaccessible part of the world ... thousands of miles from my headquarters. Yet with one movement of my finger I can reach out ..." and he pressed a small red button on the console before him "... and destroy it!"

Even as they watched, the signpost was blown to pieces by a huge rocket.

"Now listen, World," the Toad continued. "Every single signpost will share the fate of that one and Chaos and its henchman, Terror, will stalk the streets unless, by tomorrow, you proclaim me – *Emperor* of the World! *Decide*! Ha, ha, ha!"

"Good grief!" said Dangermouse.

"You've got to stop him, D.M.," growled the Colonel. "With all the signposts gone no-one will know where they've been or where they're going!"

"Don't worry, Colonel! We'll save the world!" promised Dangermouse.

"I'm sure he will!" volunteered Penfold – seldom known to volunteer for anything.

In seconds they were speeding through the air in the Mark III.

Meanwhile, on an island hideaway somewhere in the Pacific Ocean, Baron Greenback was calling a Council of Evil to order from the head of a huge black basalt table round which were grouped some of the most evil-looking scum that ever sold their grannies.

"Order, order!" called the Toad, "To business! By tomorrow, I shall be Emperor of the World – and *you* shall be my generals! To each of ..."

But before he could finish, Nero broke in with a high-pitched chatter.

"What is it, Nero?" asked Greenback – and the caterpillar indicated a television screen set into the wall.

"Ah!" breathed the Baron. "Gentlemen – we have visitors! Observe the screen! Activate camera six!"

Onto the screen came a picture of a carefully parked Mark III.

"That machine looks familiar. Switch to camera eight! As I thought, that misbegotten Dangermouse and his assinine assistant, Penfold!"

At this, a murmur of fear ran through the evil consortium.

"Don't worry Gentlemen," smiled Greenback, greasily, "it's cabaret time! I shall begin my performance as Emperor of the World ... with the Execution of Dangermouse!"

Meanwhile, unaware of the evil that was being directed against them, our heroes were scanning a huge black basalt cliff. Dangermouse turned to his assistant.

"Right, Penfold, let's see if you've been doing your homework. What does a secret agent do when he knows there's a hidden entrance but can't see it?"

"Well, he could say," started Penfold, then stopped. "You'll laugh!"

"No, I won't!" promised the White Wonder adamantly.

"You *will*!"

"Penfold! I will *not laugh*!"

"Well" ventured the diminutive hamster. "He'd say 'Open Sesame'!"

"Ha, ha, ha, ha, ha!" roared Dangermouse. "Open Ses ..."

But his words were cut short as a huge black basalt door in the cliff wall opened.

"Ah! Oh!" he smiled uneasily. "Yes yes, quite right, Penfold, he would."

Then, leaping into the Mark III he drove through into a huge black basalt cavern. As he did so, the huge black basalt door swung to behind them.

The Toad watched evilly.

"Excellent!" he grinned. "Into the mousetrap! And *so* nice of him to join in our little party game!"

The car slid to a halt before another huge black basalt door on which a sign read: "Secret Door. Give password".

"Another secret entrance!" said Penfold.

"Yes," smiled our hero. "But it's easy when you know the password. Open Sesame!" The door remained unopened. "Ah!" he went on. "Ahem! Open Sesame! ... please? Come on, Sesame! Open! Oh, good grie ..."

He broke off as, instead of being admitted, the car was abruptly propelled upwards by the release of a giant spring.

"I think," panted Dangermouse, "Greenback knows we're here, Penfold. We'll have to watch out for his tricks!"

"I wish Newton had been wrong, chief!" said Penfold dolefully.

"How d'you mean?"

"We're falling!"

"Aaaagh!"

Moments later they were standing beside the heap of tangled metal that had been the Mark III.

"Do you think you can fix it?" asked Penfold examining the wreckage.

"Can I *fix* it?" smiled Dangermouse. "Do you need to ask? I'll fix the Baron! Has he any *idea* what a respray costs?!"

In the darkness of that awesome tunnel, the imperilled pair paused and panted – but not for long. With a cry of despair Penfold dropped suddenly out of sight as a trapdoor opened beneath his feet. "Aaagh!" he yelled. "Oh 'eck! Oh fiddle! Oh crumbs!!"

"Don't worry!" Dangermouse shouted after him, "I'll come up with something!"

Then, with a leap of hope in his heart, Dangermouse spotted a descending staircase in the corner of the tunnel.

Minutes later, a supremely fit Dangermouse was gasping for breath in front of a control panel with a single red button. Over it, a sign read: "Landing platform – press button".

"What a stroke of luck! This will solve

Penfold's little problem!" he gasped.

As he pressed the button, a thickly sprung mattress shot out from the wall, ready to receive the hapless Penfold.

Less fortunately, another trap-door opened at the same time – beneath *Dangermouse's* feet. He glanced at the darkness below him:

"Mmm," he murmured. "Pity I have to leave before old Penfold gets here! Waaaaagh!" He shot into the darkness.

And, as his chief departed, Penfold arrived and bounced on the mattress before a door marked "Lift".

"Ooo! I wish Dangermouse was here! I think I'll look upstairs." He pressed the call-button and the doors slid open.

"Ah! Second floor plea . . ." he began – but his words froze in the air as a hideous slobbering monster reached out a cold, shiny hand. He tried to contain the rising panic within him:

". . . Oo! Cor! Don't panic, Penfold – what would DM do at a time like this?" Then he remembered: "I know! . . . He'd run! Aaaaaaagh!"

He ran like one possessed – if not like two possessed – or possibly just the one but re-possessed. Through endless corridors, over gaping chasms, between grasping fingers until his way was blocked by a sort of pale cerise – well, more geranium, really – door which, try as he would, he could not open.

At last, in despair, he fell gasping against it – and as it opened he fell through and down and down and down a flight of seemingly endless steps.

Meanwhile Dangermouse was completely in the dark.

"Hmmm!" he thought, "I think I'll see what a match will do! Things usually look better in the light."

But there, in the flickering light was a yellow-fanged troll.

". . . Or worse." observed our hero – and ran as fast as he could!

At last he slowed – desperately needing rest – and almost disbelievingly his outstretched hand felt . . . a bench!

"Ah!" he panted – for it was a short pant – "I'll just take the weight off my . . ."

But, when bright lights snapped on he saw he was in a cunning trap.

The seat was a tomb-like slab, strong straps anchored his body to it and over his head hung a strangely sinister device.

"Oh good grief!" sighed our hero. "It just isn't my day!"

Sniggered the evil genius, "The day is *mine*! Hee, hee, hee! The *world* is mine! Mine, *all* mine! Ha, ha, ha, ha, ha!"

"Keep smiling, Greenback!" said Dangermouse, through gritted teeth. "When I get out of here, you'll need a sense of humour!"

"Get out?" responded the toad. "You will *never* get out! But I'll make it painless – if you tell me all the classified information you know!"

"What? Betray my friends? Never!"

"Oh, but you will!" the Baron grinned evilly. "Either you *give* me the information – or I *take* it!"

And with those sinister words, Greenback reached out a gruesome finger and flicked a switch. There was a distant humming and then, oh horror, the device over Dangermouse's head began descending.

"This is my Neuro-tronic Brain Drainer!" explained the arch villain. "In seconds it will remove every thought you ever had between your ears!"

As he spoke, the lonely white figure on the slab twitched and jerked convulsively.

"Soon we shall be in his inner sanctum – and we shall see his deepest secrets!" said Greenback with glee.

But, whatever he had expected, what he *saw* was a large placard which read: "Not this time, Baron!"

"Huh?" snarled the Beastly Toad. "So his feeble mind is resisting? Then I shall *increase* the power!"

As the current flowed, DM's fingers beat a wild tattoo and his nose gleamed faintly.

"Ugh! Agh! Umm! . . ." he panted.

"Now we shall see!" cackled the Baron –

but what he saw was another message: "Try again fatty!"

"Still he resists!" Greenback cursed. "In vain, wretched rodent, for no-one can resist – *full power*!"

Now the hum of the devilish device grew to a terrifying growl, DM's eyelids fluttered like a wounded frog and his nose flashed alternately red, white and blue.

After several seconds, the brain-drain device sputtered, fizzed, and finally exploded in a shower of sparks. Dangermouse burst his bonds and sat up.

"Ah! Always feel better for 40 winks!"

The watching villains shook slightly and Nero uttered a high-pitched whine.

"Ah yes, my dear Nero," comforted the Baron, "but we shall have his beloved assistant." He called to the sound-sensitive panel on the wall.

The screen flickered once more – and Penfold appeared, creeping along.

"Good! Good!" chuckled the evil genius. "Now, poor straying simpleton ... I think he needs a little pick-me-up!"

At that, a hairy hand the size of a wheelbarrow seized the fleeing hamster. With a shriek ... "Wow-ow-ow!" ... he was hauled upwards until the viewers could see him no more.

"How very amusing! Hee, hee, hee!" chortled the Baron and, moments later, the struggling wretch was suspended above a pit from whose terrifying depths leapt a savage, toothy, lip-smacking, crocodile!

Dangermouse was creeping through the black basalt tunnel when he heard a scream of cowardly terror.

"Hum!" he pondered. "A scream of cowardly terror ... must be Penfold! Better see what the problem is!

Penfold was in the last stages of quivering fear and had given himself up for lost when, abruptly, a white figure cut an arc in the air, his chains were snapped by an almost mystic force and he found himself in his hero's arms once more!

Then, as he gazed into the pit that he had thought would be his doom, the crocodile reached out a knobbly claw and delicately placed a lighted bomb beside them.

"Hmmm!" observed Dangermouse. "Doesn't look a patch on Blackpool illuminations. I think we'll leave!" And, with

that, the perspicacious pair fled once more.

"Excellent!" hissed the hidden watcher. "Out of the frying pan into ... the fire.".

In the depths of that black prison, Penfold suddenly left DM's side.

He had little choice, since giant pincers had seized him by the ear and plucked him skywards before he could say "crikey!".

At the same time, the White Wonder was beset with deadly shafts of laser light from every angle. He ducked, he dodged; he jumped, he jigged; he leapt to the left, ran to the right and stood on his head.

"What a performance, Nero!" exclaimed the Toad. "Very like Fred Astaire, don't you think?"

Just then Dangermouse made an astounding leap between two, intersecting beams, hit the pincer release button and *almost* caught Penfold as he fell ...

"Curse him!" grated Greenback from his lair. "One last chance, Dangermouse, your freedom for all your secrets!"

But Dangermouse, standing proudly beside a crumpled Penfold only said:

"Never!"

"Oh chief!" whimpered his assistant. "It's not a bad off..."

But he never had a chance to finish – as so often before, a trap-door opened beneath them and together they plunged into a gaping chasm. In a second though, Dangermouse was on his feet.

"I said – never!! You can do what you like but ..."

But he never had time to finish – as so often before a huge four ton weight fell on him from on high and sent them both to an even lower, even blacker dungeon.

"Nero!" shrieked the Baron, "I've beaten him! The moment I've dreamed of! This is the end, Dangermouse ..."

And so, indeed it seemed. Both the world's greatest secret agent and his assistant were exhausted; the sides of the deep, dark dungeon were sheer and shiny – and they were surrounded by 137 tons of dynamite about to be triggered by a clock whose fingers were ticking away the last few seconds to oblivion ...

"You fiend!" called Dangermouse, stoutly. "You black-hearted no good, monstrous, evil scheming, treacherous megalomaniacle misfit!"

"Oh – pretty!" giggled Greenback. "But flattery won't save you – your time is up!"

The victims' eyes turned to the clock – 4 ... 3 ... 2 ... 1 ... As the clock reached zero, Dangermouse screamed.

"Had a nice nap, chief ?" said Penfold as he dusted the sofa in the flat.

"Nice nap?" said a dazed Dangermouse. "But what about ... ?"

Before he could finish, Colonel K's face was talking to him from the video screen.

"Ah! DM! Look here, DM! Chaos and terror are stalking the ... er ... DM? Are you listening to me?" Dangermouse turned with a puzzled frown:

"Oh! Yes, Colonel, sorry!"

"It's that devil Greenback again. You'll never dream what he's up to ..."

"Threatening to throw the world into chaos and confusion ..." said Dangermouse.

"Amazing!" gasped Colonel K. "How did you know?"

"... by destroying every important signpost in the world?" went on our hero.

"By George that's – that's absolutely right! You a telepath DM?"

"No, sir, a mouse!" DM responded. "But don't worry, Penfold and I will stop him! Come on Penfold!!"

In no time at all they were winging over the city in the Mark III.

"'Ere, chief !" squeaked Penfold. "You never asked him where we have to go!"

"I know where the Baron's hideout is!" answered the White Wonder. "Oh, and *this* time, mind the crocodile!"

"Crocodile! *What* crocodile?"

"The big green one with the sharp teeth that tries to eat you on page 57."

"Oo 'eck!" said a worried Penfold. "I don't like the sound of this! Where's it all go going to end?"

"I would say," said Dangermouse. "On page 59."

– And it did!

TRACKING IN THE COUNTRY

Penfold rather enjoys tracking. He gets very nervous in cars so tailing the enemy on foot suits him down to the ground.

Tell-tale Clues

When you track someone notice everything around you. Disturbed birds show that your quarry is somewhere nearby. If *you* scare the birds it probably means he didn't go that way. You've taken a wrong turn.

Thorns and barbed wire often catch threads from clothing. Dead leaves, when disturbed, can overturn and reveal their darker, moist side. This is usually a sign that someone has passed recently.

Every so often stand still – look and listen! If you're downwind to your quarry sounds carry clearly.

Never get too close unless you're out for a capture. If you are shadowing, do little more than keep him in sight.

Avoid Being Spotted

As far as possible never leave cover yourself. Move from one cover point to another, making use of shadow, bushes, trees and any dry ditch. Wear soft shoes that won't make a noise – trainers are excellent.

Duck, crouch – even crawl if necessary. Never stand to full height on the skyline – you'll stick out like a sore thumb. Avoid sunlit patches. It's better to lose a little time by avoiding them than risk being seen.

Never wear anything likely to reflect. Be particularly cautious if your quarry has a dog. It may easily scent you even if you are unseen. If possible stay downwind.

Finding Your Bearings

It is most important to make sure you don't get lost and can find your way back. Every good agent should carry a compass, but don't worry if you find yourself out in the country without one. There are other ways.

Note every landmark – church towers, unusual trees. They will help you on your way back – only then they'll be on the other side.

Making a Compass

There is another way of getting your bearings without a compass, if you have a watch – and provided it is sunny.

Hold your watch flat, face upwards, so the sun shines on it. Turn it round until the *hour hand* points at the sun.

Without moving the watch, place a pencil across the dial as shown, so it rests on the centre and points halfway between 12 and the hour hand. The line made by the pencil will be a true north/south line.

Footprints

Look for and study footprints, particularly in loose earth, mud, sand or snow. If water is in them, or if they look dry and cracked, they are probably old and not made by your quarry.

Footprints can tell quite a story. If they are complete – with heel and toe – your quarry is walking unhurriedly.

The prints will be closer together if your quarry is running. Fast running will leave only toeprints.

There's more cover, more people, less risk of drawing attention than in the country.

But shop windows reflect and a careful quarry may use them as mirrors. He can saunter past yet check out anything suspicious happening behind.

Wear nothing to draw attention or make you stand out. Your job is to merge into the background.

If your quarry stops, don't you stop immediately. Carry on a few paces, stroll into a shop. (Dratted Penfold! He's shot in to buy bickies again!)

Don't stare at your target. Always keep other moving people between you.

Cross the road sometimes. It might be easier to keep pace from the other side.

Try to anticipate his moves. If he suddenly runs, you know that you've blown it. Don't leap across before traffic.

Never make sudden moves which might draw attention.

Once you have been noticed, even though your quarry may not recognise you, he is more likely to notice you again.

He'll grow wary, and you're likely to lose him.

It's often better if you and a fellow agent can work together, one getting ahead of the quarry and the second following.

I often do this with Penfold. WHERE IS HE? Don't tell me he's just got himself lost!

TRACKING IN THE TOWN

Shaking a Tail

Penfold, once dragged from the litter basket, has had another rush of brains to the head.

"WHAT IF *YOU* ARE FOLLOWED?" he nervously asks. (That's why he dived in the basket.)

Good point, Penfold! The tracker tracked is a tricky situation. I usually take precautions in advance.

A folded cap in your pocket and a pair of glasses (not worn normally) are easily carried.

Step into a busy shop or store, slip on hat and glasses and slip out with people just leaving.

It may not dawn on your "shadow" for two or three minutes, which is all the start you need.

Underground Stations provide another excellent means of losing a follower, particularly if the station is busy.

The best way is to gain cover and remain perfectly still. Never run for the cover or allow your tracker to think that you've noticed him. Keep your cool!

Hide and do not make a sound. He'll have lost sight of you, he'll be worried.

Never choose the most obvious hiding-place, for so will he. His anxious searching elsewhere may be your chance to slip quietly away.

Laying a Trail

You obviously can't use sticks or stones in town. It's hard to find any and they would probably be knocked away as people walk past.

If you need to leave signs for your contact to follow use chalk on the pavement or on fences.

1
2
3
4
5
6
7
8
9

TRICKY TRACKS

OK, agents! Let's see how good you are at tracking. Work out who or what made all these tracks.

Answers are on page 78.

DANGER MOUSE
MUSHROOMS ON THE MARCH
IN THE PALE GREY LIGHT OF A FEBRUARY MORNING, LONDON WAS STIRRING.
ARE YOU GOIN' TO BE ALL DAY WITH THAT TEASPOON, MR. LONDON?
HAS THE MILKMAN BEEN YET? WE'VE RUN OUT OF MILK.
SILLY FOOL OF A MILKMAN'S LEFT ME A BASKET OF MUSHROO....
LONDON LOOKED UP AND GASPED IN HORROR.....
AAAGH!
A DAY OR TWO AFTER THIS, IN THE SECRET CONFINES OF A MAYFAIR PILLAR-BOX, PENFOLD HAD JUST PREPARED A PLATEFUL OF BACON SANDWICHES.
WASN'T THAT THE VIDEO TELEPHONE ALARM? PENFOLD? TUT! DOZING ON THE RUG AGAIN?
BEST BACK BACON LOVELY AND CRISP..
BLAST! WHY DO I KEEP GETTING 'CORONATION STREET' ON THIS WRETCHED THING? AH D.M. PROBLEM FOR YOU! PENFOLD ABOUT?
HE'S ON THE MAT, COLONEL.
I'VE GOT MUSHROOMS ON ME MIND!
HMM, PROBABLY THE DAMP WEATHER, COLONEL?
I MEAN, THAT THE WORLD IS THREATENED BY MUSHROOMS! HERRUMPH! GIANT FUNGI, MARCHIN' INTO PEOPLE'S HOMES, HYPNOTISIN' THEM AND LEAVIN' THEM LIKE ZOMBIES WITH WILD, STARIN' EYES TALKIN' TOTAL GIBBERISH!
GOOD GRIEF, SIR! THEN I'D BETTER CANCEL MY THEATRE TICKETS AND SAVE THE WORLD! SHAME, THOUGH, I ALWAYS ENJOY 'THE MOUSETRAP'!

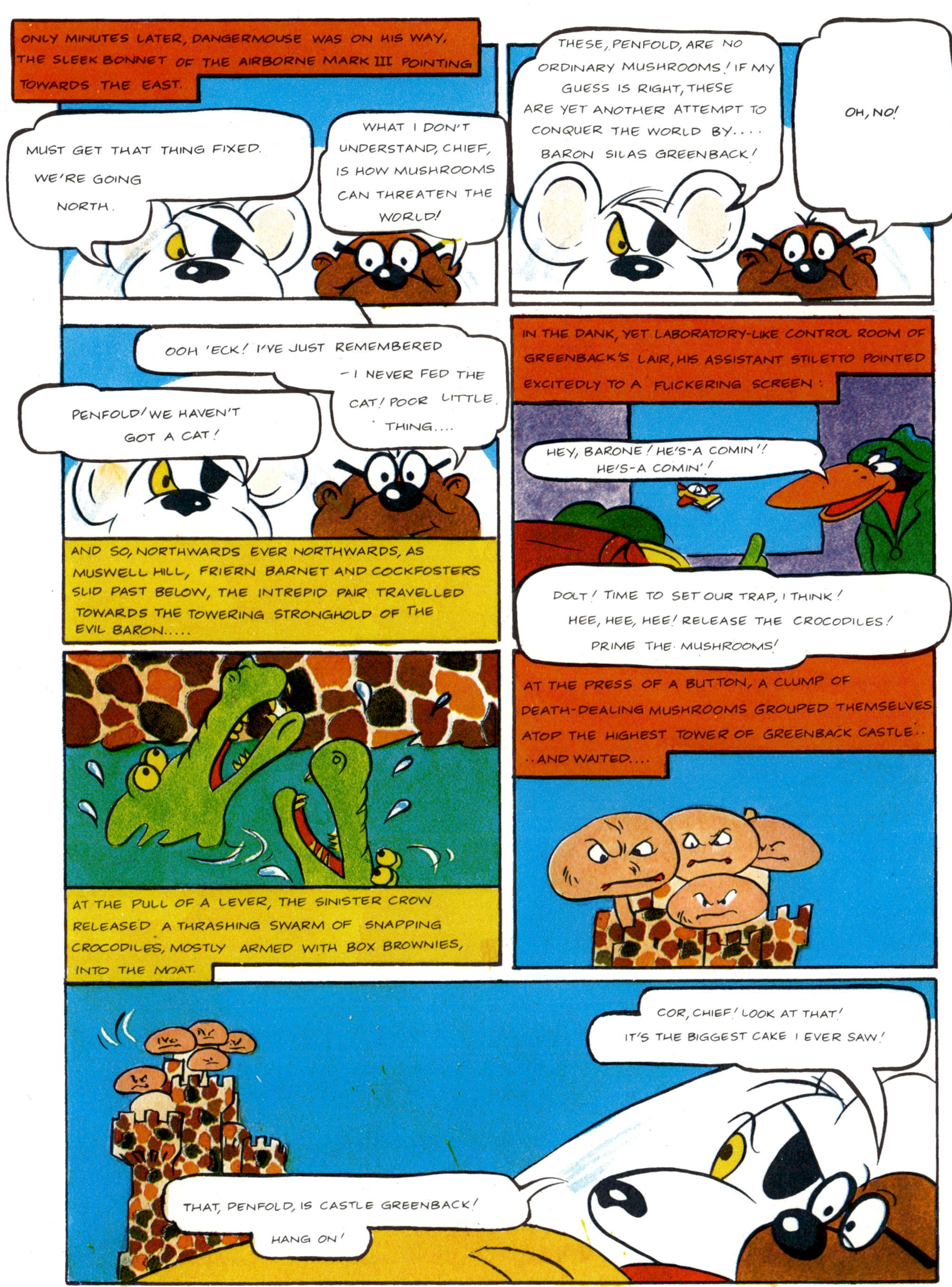
ONLY MINUTES LATER, DANGERMOUSE WAS ON HIS WAY, THE SLEEK BONNET OF THE AIRBORNE MARK III POINTING TOWARDS THE EAST.
MUST GET THAT THING FIXED. WE'RE GOING NORTH.
WHAT I DON'T UNDERSTAND, CHIEF, IS HOW MUSHROOMS CAN THREATEN THE WORLD!
THESE, PENFOLD, ARE NO ORDINARY MUSHROOMS! IF MY GUESS IS RIGHT, THESE ARE YET ANOTHER ATTEMPT TO CONQUER THE WORLD BY.... BARON SILAS GREENBACK!
OH, NO!
OOH 'ECK! I'VE JUST REMEMBERED – I NEVER FED THE CAT! POOR LITTLE THING....
PENFOLD! WE HAVEN'T GOT A CAT!
AND SO, NORTHWARDS EVER NORTHWARDS, AS MUSWELL HILL, FRIERN BARNET AND COCKFOSTERS SLID PAST BELOW, THE INTREPID PAIR TRAVELLED TOWARDS THE TOWERING STRONGHOLD OF THE EVIL BARON.....
IN THE DANK, YET LABORATORY-LIKE CONTROL ROOM OF GREENBACK'S LAIR, HIS ASSISTANT STILETTO POINTED EXCITEDLY TO A FLICKERING SCREEN:
HEY, BARONE! HE'S-A COMIN'! HE'S-A COMIN'!
DOLT! TIME TO SET OUR TRAP, I THINK! HEE, HEE, HEE! RELEASE THE CROCODILES! PRIME THE MUSHROOMS!
AT THE PULL OF A LEVER, THE SINISTER CROW RELEASED A THRASHING SWARM OF SNAPPING CROCODILES, MOSTLY ARMED WITH BOX BROWNIES, INTO THE MOAT.
AT THE PRESS OF A BUTTON, A CLUMP OF DEATH-DEALING MUSHROOMS GROUPED THEMSELVES ATOP THE HIGHEST TOWER OF GREENBACK CASTLE.. ..AND WAITED....
COR, CHIEF! LOOK AT THAT! IT'S THE BIGGEST CAKE I EVER SAW!
THAT, PENFOLD, IS CASTLE GREENBACK! HANG ON!

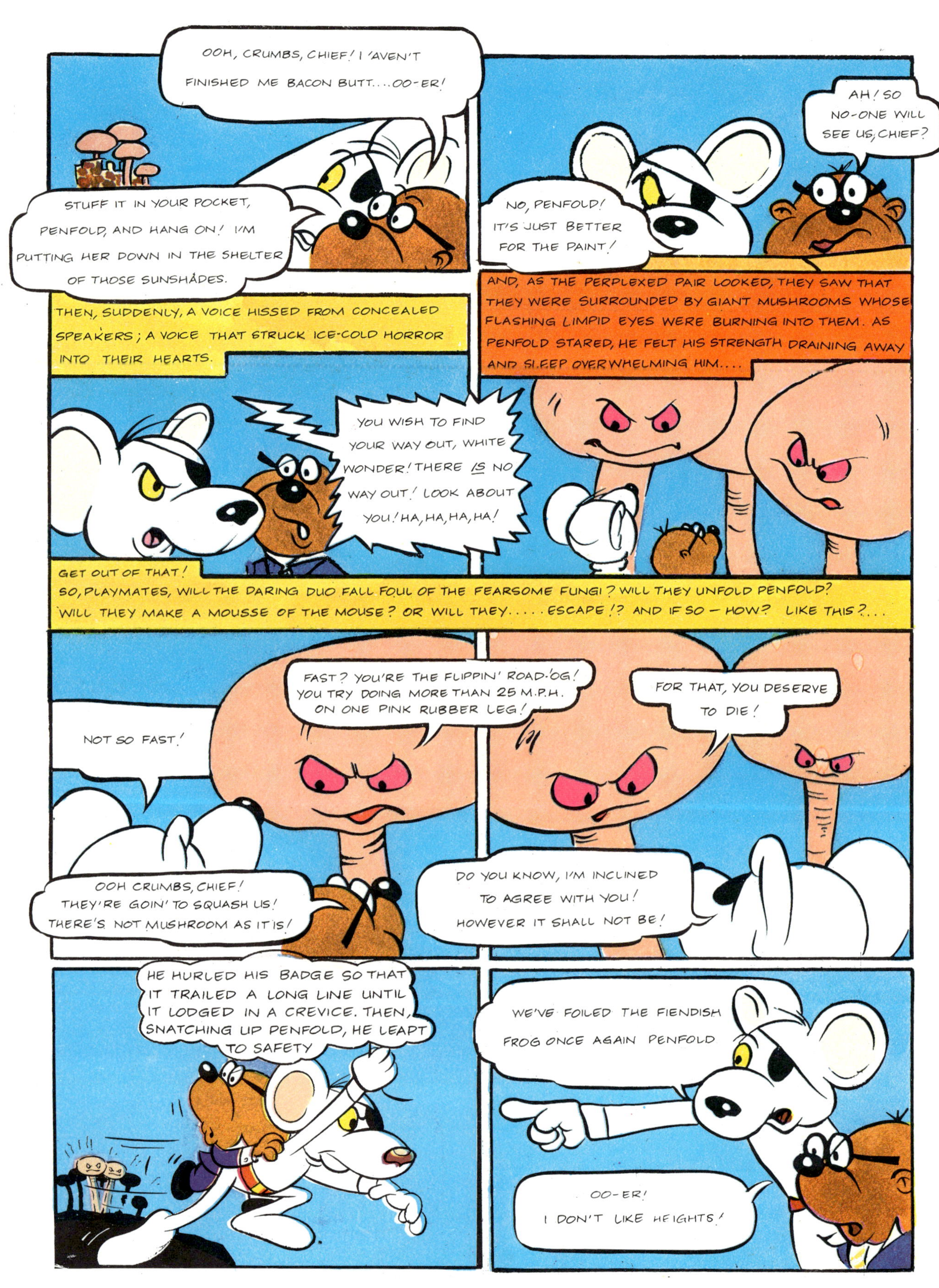
OOH, CRUMBS, CHIEF! I 'AVEN'T FINISHED ME BACON BUTT....OO-ER!
STUFF IT IN YOUR POCKET, PENFOLD, AND HANG ON! I'M PUTTING HER DOWN IN THE SHELTER OF THOSE SUNSHADES.
AH! SO NO-ONE WILL SEE US, CHIEF?
NO, PENFOLD! IT'S JUST BETTER FOR THE PAINT!
THEN, SUDDENLY, A VOICE HISSED FROM CONCEALED SPEAKERS; A VOICE THAT STRUCK ICE-COLD HORROR INTO THEIR HEARTS.
YOU WISH TO FIND YOUR WAY OUT, WHITE WONDER! THERE IS NO WAY OUT! LOOK ABOUT YOU! HA, HA, HA, HA!
AND, AS THE PERPLEXED PAIR LOOKED, THEY SAW THAT THEY WERE SURROUNDED BY GIANT MUSHROOMS WHOSE FLASHING LIMPID EYES WERE BURNING INTO THEM. AS PENFOLD STARED, HE FELT HIS STRENGTH DRAINING AWAY AND SLEEP OVERWHELMING HIM....
GET OUT OF THAT!
SO, PLAYMATES, WILL THE DARING DUO FALL FOUL OF THE FEARSOME FUNGI? WILL THEY UNFOLD PENFOLD? WILL THEY MAKE A MOUSSE OF THE MOUSE? OR WILL THEY.....ESCAPE!? AND IF SO — HOW? LIKE THIS?...
NOT SO FAST!
FAST? YOU'RE THE FLIPPIN' ROAD-'OG! YOU TRY DOING MORE THAN 25 M.P.H. ON ONE PINK RUBBER LEG!
OOH CRUMBS, CHIEF! THEY'RE GOIN' TO SQUASH US! THERE'S NOT MUSHROOM AS IT IS!
FOR THAT, YOU DESERVE TO DIE!
DO YOU KNOW, I'M INCLINED TO AGREE WITH YOU! HOWEVER IT SHALL NOT BE!
HE HURLED HIS BADGE SO THAT IT TRAILED A LONG LINE UNTIL IT LODGED IN A CREVICE. THEN, SNATCHING UP PENFOLD, HE LEAPT TO SAFETY
WE'VE FOILED THE FIENDISH FROG ONCE AGAIN PENFOLD
OO-ER! I DON'T LIKE HEIGHTS!

OR LIKE THIS?....
HOLD IT, HOLD IT? WIV WHAT, MAY I ASK? WE ARE MUSHROOMS, YOU KNOW! WE'RE NOT FLIPPIN' OCTOPUSES!
HOLD IT RIGHT THERE!
PEA!
MUSHROOM!
NO, I MEAN OCTOPI!
KEEP THEM TALKING, PENFOLD! WHILE I EMPTY YOUR TURN-UPS!
MY TURN-UPS!
I THOUGHT WE WERE TALKING ABOUT PEAS!
I NEED THE FLUFF!
YE SPOTTED SNAKES WITH DOUBLE TONGUE COME NOT NEAR OUR FAIRY QUEEN!
WHAT? SPOTTED SNAKES! YOU EVER SEEN A SPOTTED SNAKE?
IT'S SHAKESPEARE!
WHAT A STUPID NAME FOR A SNAKE!
WHILE THE ARGUMENT WENT ON, DANGERMOUSE DEXTEROUSLY REMOVED THE FLUFF, CRUMBS, COPPER SULPHATE AND HYDRATED LIME FROM PENFOLD'S TURN-UPS. SPINNING HIS NOSE AT PRECISELY 2.461 R.P.M. HE BLENDED THEM SKILFULLY WITH THE CONTENTS OF HIS HIP FLASK.
WITH ONE SWIFT CIRCULAR MOVEMENT OF HIS POWERFUL SLEEVE, HE SCATTERED THE LETHAL MIXTURE OVER THE BEMUSED MUSHROOMS. GASPING, THEY WILTED, STAGGERED, AND FELL....
AAGH! OOOH! WAAAGH!
THAT WAS A POWERFUL LOT OF FUNGICIDE!
I DON'T THINK GREENBACK WILL FIND IT FUNNY! HEE! HEE!

ANSWERS:

WAS IT NO. 1?	NO! AS ANY DEVOTED STUDENT OF DM WOULD KNOW, HIS LIFE-LINE WOULD BE 3·7 cm TOO SHORT TO REACH THE PINNACLE – BESIDES, WHERE WOULD HE GO FROM THERE?
WAS IT NO. 2?	OH COME ON! YOURE NOT TAKING THIS BOOK SERIOUSLY ARE YOU?
WAS IT NO. 3?	OFCOURSE IT WAS! READ IT AND SEE!

SECRET CODES

It is vital for any agent to learn a few secret codes – in fact, the more you know the better. If you are able to vary the code you use for sending messages to fellow agents it will make deciphering them more difficult for your enemies.

Any code is a system of signs, symbols, numbers or letters which allow you to pass on information in the most secretive way. It is a good idea to make yourself a code book listing all the codes that you and your fellow spies use. You can refer to this when coding or decoding messages.

It is, of course, vital that this is kept in a secure place. If your enemies get hold of your code book you will have to start from scratch with a new set of codes.

Secret codes are not a new invention. As long ago as 450 BC the artful Spartans were writing secret messages. Their method was both ingenious and simple.

One general would take a long, thin strip of parchment and wrap it tightly around his staff, making sure the edges met perfectly all the way round. He then wrote his message along the joined edges, each letter being half on one side of a join and half on the other. The strip was then unrolled and sent to wherever it was needed.

The commander receiving it would roll the length of parchment onto a staff identical to that used by the writer. The letters again became whole revealing their message. This method was known as the Transposition Cipher. Once the method was known it became very easy to break.

Julius Caesar used another kind of cipher, the Substitution Cipher. By making the 4th letter of the alphabet stand for the 1st, the 5th for the 2nd and so on he had a simple code that was much more difficult to break than the Spartan cipher.

In biblical times the old tribes formed a cipher by reversing the order of their alphabet.

During England's Civil War the art of the cipher really took off. King Charles I was an expert and some of his messages held their secrets until the 19th Century! Our wily ancestors used many methods. Here are a few of them.

Superfluous words or letters were put into some innocent letter in which most of the writing was "padding". It was previously agreed that words at certain set intervals formed the real message. All the rest was so much camouflage.

In another letter the true "punch line" could only be detected by reading vertically or diagonally (or following any simple design already agreed). If you try this method be careful to write neatly so there is no confusion over which letters line up. Practise on graph paper.

Sometimes secret messages are written entirely with numbers. It is quite easy to make up a number code. You can use a code wheel – which is explained on page 73 or you can simply work out a substitution cipher – A = 1, B = 2 etc. would be the easiest. It's also the easiest to break! Whatever code you devise don't forget to write it in your code book for future reference.

Penfold is already beginning to reel at the thought of all these ciphers. The only thing he is any good at deciphering is a menu!

I bet you already see the possibilities of forming codes of your own. Take the method that most appeals to you and experiment. But remember, your fellow agent who receives your message needs to know the code you are using. Make sure you have identical code books and a means of indicating which code is being used. Give them all innocent names that can be incorporated into the message. You could number them and put the number instead of the date at the top of your letter.

The Campbell Code

Simply substitute shapes for letters – a very simple code. You can make your message look like a decorative border at the top of a letter!

Good grief! What has Penfold written?

Answer on p. 78

Dangermorse Code

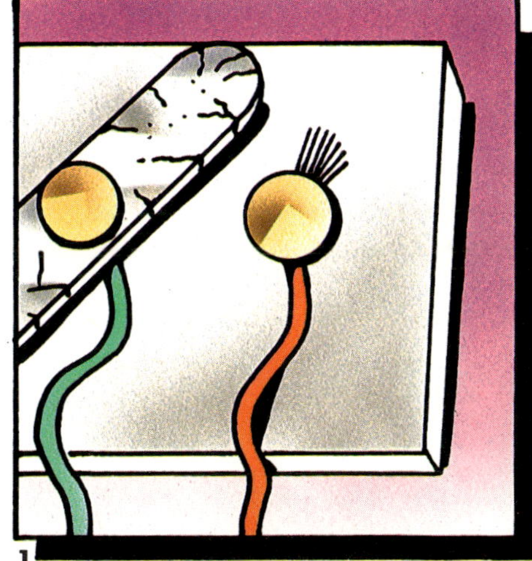
1.

2.

Morse is an internationally known code used for transmitting messages by radio from ships. It consists simply of dots and dashes – a dash being equal in length to three dots. A gap equal to one dot is left between each of the symbols, twice as much between letters and a longer pause between words.

Morse can also be transmitted by flashing a light. You can make a transmitter quite easily. This is Colonel K's version, invented by the infamous double agent Nicholaiski.

A piece of wood 60 × 100 mm
2 drawing pins
1 ice-lolly stick covered in aluminium foil
3 250 mm lengths of bell wire (preferably green, red and yellow)
1 batten-type lamp holder and pocket torch bulb
A 4.5 volt battery

1. Pin the lolly stick onto the wood with a drawing pin as shown. Attach the green wire to the pin. Stick the other drawing pin into the wood and attach the red wire to it.
2. Attach the other end of the green wire to the + terminal of the battery and attach the other end of the red wire to the lamp holder. Attach the yellow wire to the – terminal and to the lamp holder.
3. The light will flash when you press the lolly stick down and make contact with the drawing pin.

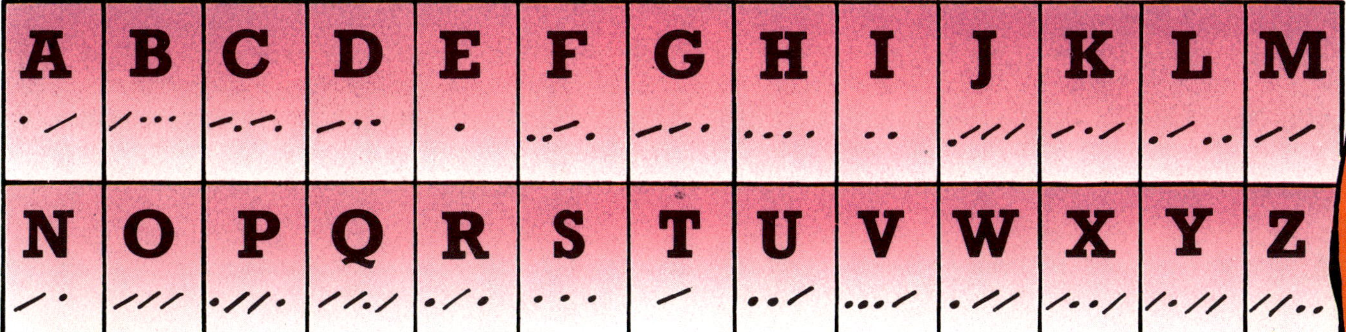

3.

Semaphore

Semaphore is very useful for passing messages to fellow agents when you are out in the country. (Penfold isn't too good at it because his arms are so short!) You can signal messages without making a sound and so avoid giving yourself away to the enemy – unless he can see you!

Signal with your arms or use flags – these are best if you are some distance away.

Always make definite movements and don't wobble your arms – it will make your message hard to read.

You can also use semaphore for written messages. Use the clockface system, putting the two "hands" into a circle so that each letter will actually look like a clockface.

A
B
C
D
E
F
G
H
I
J
K
L
M
N
O
P
Q
R
S
T
U
V
W
X
Y
Z

The Code Wheel

A code wheel is most useful because you can make a great number of codes with it.

You need two circles of card, one should be 20 mm larger in diameter than the other.

Divide the circumference of each circle into 26 equal parts, putting the letters of the alphabet on the outer rim and numbers 1–26 on the inner rim.

Make a hole through the centre of each circle and fasten them together.

You agree beforehand which number will be substituted for A. In this case it is 5, so **DM** would be **8 17**. You could move the wheel and change all the numbers if you wish.

By varying the codes in this way you make them harder to break.

Breaking Ciphers

For once Penfold and I agree. It is dodgy, definitely dodgy! Old Greenback's no genius (though he *thinks* he is), but unless you have some idea of which code he is using you can spend hours – or in Penfold's case, days – breaking it.

The first thing you do is to look for the symbol or letter used most frequently in the enemy message – in English it will correspond to the letter E. This gives you a start – put in all the Es. T is the next most frequent letter.

The order of frequency for the rest of the alphabet is as follows A, O, N, I, R, S, H, D, L, C, W, U, M, F, Y, G, V, K, Q, X, J, Z.

All single letters are likely to be A, O or I. The most common double letters are EE, OO, FF, LL, SS.

Two letter words are easy to work out. They will be IF, AS, AT, BY, IS, OF, TO, HE, IT, IN etc.

Working from this and from your knowledge of codes you now use your head to decide what the message is likely to be about. No, Penfold, it *won't* be a recipe for Bacon Butties! It may tell you where a DROP is to be made, or where a MEET will be.

It may include a time – either in numbers or lettered code. So if a number crops up in the middle of a jumble of letters and symbols, it's quite likely to be a time.

Try to put yourself in the position of your enemies and ask yourself what is the most *likely* kind of message. What kind of mission do you suspect they are working on?

It's like doing a puzzle – you keep trying the possibilities until something makes sense.

Perhaps you would like to try your hand at deciphering. Penfold has completely given up on this one. It would be understandable it if was a message from Greenback that he had intercepted. But these are his orders from Colonel K! Even with his code book he can't work them out! I'm sure you spies will fare better. I'll give you one clue. The Colonel is using a code from this book.

11 22 9 9 18 6 5 7 8
20 16 5 18 18 13 18 11
6 5 7 19 18
6 25 24 24 3
12 13 14 5 7 15
15

Dear John
Susan and I will both meet you tomorrow. We can't come tonight but we will be reddy at four o'clock. meet us at 7 Heath Green Road - Susan's house - by the station entrance, next to Oaktree Avenue.

see you soon Tom

John and Tom have agreed that every 6th word will make up a message. Can you work out the message in the letter?

Answers are on page 78.

A Message from Dangermouse

Becoming a super secret agent isn't easy. You will really have to work at it. I've given you all the basics in this book and now it's up to you to perfect your disguise, learn your secret codes and train your fellow agents. (I've been training Penfold for years and he still makes mistakes.)

Check how you did in all the quizzes. If you got every one right then you are already a superspy. Try out your new skills with the Superspy Skills Quiz on the next page. This is a **real** test of your ingenuity.

If you become a highly skilled agent who knows—maybe Colonel K will ask you to join our ranks.

Dangermouse

Your Secret Dossier

Name ______________________

Code Name ______________________

Spy Ring Name ______________________

Rank (Director, spy, cut out) ______________________

Password ______________________

Rendezvous Points ______________________

Fellow Spies **Code names** ______________________

____

____

____

____

____

Answers

Spot the Spies
There are 9 spies on the station. The "blind" man is looking at his watch. A small boy is pulling a false beard off a spy. Two identical spies are carrying identical bags – obviously about to switch them. The porter is photographing luggage labels. Another man is talking into his buttonhole – in reality a transmitter. One spy is slipping a message into another spy's pocket. The lady buying flowers has a tape recorder in her basket.

The hidden objects are a tape recorder, camera, binoculars, gun, radio set, secret file and a transmitter.

Which did *you* think was the *real* Greenback? It's really quite obvious. There's only one Nero so it has to be the Scottish Greenback. Any good spy would have known that!

Tricky Tracks
1 Stiletto, 2 horse, 3 Penfold, 4 bicycle, 5 Nero, 6 duckling, 7 duck, 8 bird, 9 Dangermouse, 10 dog, 11 Greenback with stick, 12 kangaroo, 13 snake, 14 Colonel K, 15 elephant.

Breaking Ciphers
Colonel K used the code wheel as shown on page 72 – A = 5 and so on. The message was: GREENBACK PLANNING BACON BUTTY HIJACK K.

The message reads: Meet tonight at 7 by oak tree (Oaktree).

The Campbell Code
Penfold's message was CHOCKY BICKIES.

SUPERSPY SKILLS QUIZ

To be a **Super Spy** you must be quick thinking, alert and resourceful. It is the unexpected emergency that sorts out the Dangermice from the Penfolds. What would you do in these situations?

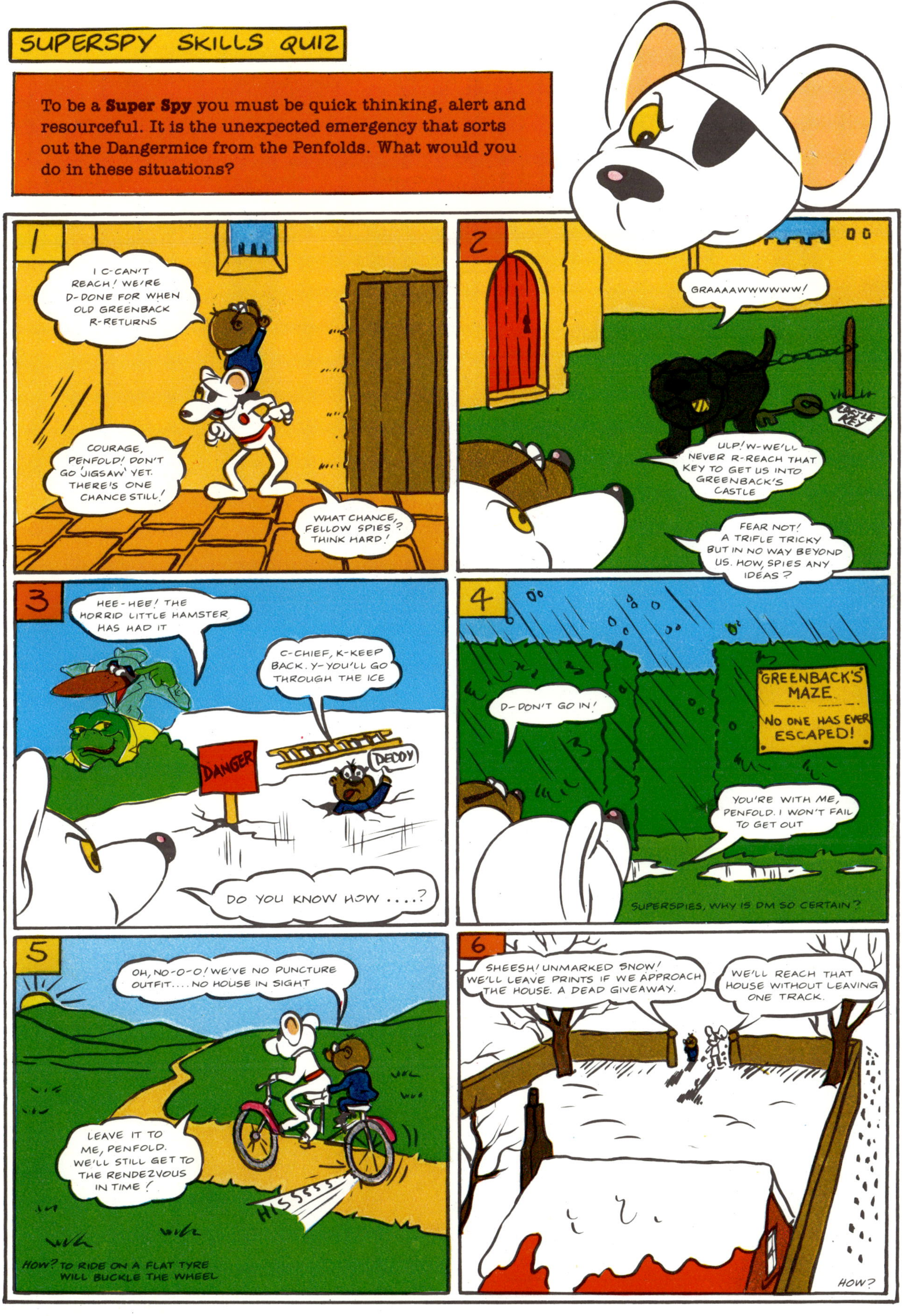

Answers

1
HURRY PENFOLD, GREENBACK'S COMING!
I'M CLIMBING AS FAST AS I CAN!
2
3
IF DM SPREADS HIS WEIGHT OVER A MUCH WIDER AREA, THE ICE WILL PROBABLY HOLD. HE KNOWS THIS AND HAS NOTICED THE LADDER.
DANGER!
4
DANGERMOUSE CAN FOLLOW HIS OWN FOOTPRINTS ON THE WAY OUT
5
DANGERMOUSE STUFFS THE TYRE WITH MOSS MAKING IT POSSIBLE TO RIDE THE BIKE
6
WHAT, YOU'VE GOT THEM ALL RIGHT? GOOD GRIEF, I'D BETTER LOOK OUT FOR MY JOB!